VALUES IN LANGUAGE TEXTBOOKS

VALUES IN LANGUAGE TEXTBOOKS

By

Dr. M. Indira Devi

M.A., M.Ed., Ph.D.
Principal
A.L. College of Education
Guntur–522 002

Editors

Dr. J. Prasanth Kumar

M.A., M.Ed., M.Phil., Ph.D.
Reader
A.L. Collged of Education
Guntur–522 002

&

Dr. Digumarti Bhaskara Rao

M.Sc., M.A., M.A., M.Ed., Ph.D.,
Reader
R.V.R. College of Education
Srinivasa Nagar Colony
Guntur–522 006
Andhra Pradesh
India

DISCOVERY PUBLISHING HOUSE
NEW DELHI-110002

First Published-2004

Reprint 2006

ISBN 81-7141-833-3

Published by

DISCOVERY PUBLISHING HOUSE
4831/24, Ansari Road, Prahlad Street,
Darya Ganj, New Delhi-110002 (India)
Phone: 23279245 • Fax: 91-11-23253475
E-mail:dphtemp@indiatimes.com

Printed at:
Tarun Offset Printers, Delhi-53

Dedicated

to the

Management

Staff

and

Students

of

A.L. College of Education

Who are There

All Around the World

in Teaching Profession

Preface

Values play a very vital role in motivating and sustaining the active and concrete contribution of a person to himself and to others. The values are developed in family as well as in educational institutions. The educational institutions, through the use of textbooks, should propagate the values needed for a person and to a society.

Identifying the very role of language textbooks in developing values, a comprehensive study has been undertaken to study the importance given to values in school language textbooks. The findings are quite interesting and useful to policy planners, educators, administrators, curriculum designers, textbook writers, teachers and parents.

Values, in educational institutions, must be preached and practised to the best to prepare good citizens.

Dr. D. B. Rao

Sai Soudha
D-43, S.V.N. Colony
Guntur–522 006
Andhra Pradesh

Contents

Preface v

1. **The Study and Its Importance** **1-23**

Aims and Values of Education, Meaning of Values, Value Education, Classification of Values, Personal Values, Social Values, National Values, Sources of Value Education

2. **Role of Textbooks and Need for the Study** **24-36**

Teaching of Language, The Role of Textbooks, Textbooks in Mother Tongue, Need and Importance of the Study, Objectives of the Study, Scope and Limitations of the Study, Explanations of the Important Terms Used

3. **Review of Related Literature** **37-59**

Studies on Values in Education in General, Studies on Values of Students, Studies on Religious Values, Studies on Moral Instruction, Studies on Democratic Values, Studies on Measurement on Educational Values, Studies on Values in Textbooks, Studies on Evaluation of Textbooks, Studies on Survey of Textbooks, Studies Abroad

4. **Method of Investigation** **60-67**

Methodology, Value Manifestation Schedule, Description of Documents

5. **Analysis and Interpretation** **68-139**

Quantitative Interpretation, Qualitative Interpretation, Moral Values, Primary Level, Secondary Level—Prose

Lessons, Secondary Level—Poetry Lessons, Secondary Level—Non-detailed Texts, Primary Level—Prose Lessons, Primary Level—Poetry Lessons, Secular Values, Conclusions, Generalisations

6. Executive Summary **140-152**

Introduction, Value Education, Classification of Values, Source of Value Education, Need for the Study, Objectives of the Study, Scope and Limitations of the Study, Review of Related Literature, Method of Investigation, Findings, Moral Value, Democratic Value, Secular Value, Conclusion, Suggestions for Further Studies

Bibliography *153*

Additional Reading *161*

Index *177*

1

The Study and Its Importance

Introduction

India believes in the possibility of a new social order, and dreams of a society built on the rich cultural heritage and values of our country. But it, must be remembered that the dreams of a new society will never be realised, unless the young people who form an integral part of the society who in the process of education have developed firm convictions, sound morals, and a clear value system.

During recent years, the growth of indiscipline, the lack of ideals, and the weakening of social and moral values in the younger generation have caused grave concern in many countries of the world including India. This is an age where for the youth the past is irrelevant, the present uncertain and the future confused and fearful. The erosion of human values today has become a strong phenomenon. There is a maddening pursuit to acquire wealth, power, and status to the total exclusion of humanness in the society. No doubt, man has travelled a long distance from the troglodyte he once was, crouching into the caverns of the earth to the modern spacemen but he does not seem to have learnt to live, so far, as a human being on this earth.

It is felt that there is a crisis of character as well as values in human life today. In this context, the University Commission Report headed by Dr. S. Radhakrishnan 1948 stressed the duty of education.

"The weakness of present generation is that it is rootless and the true function of a university is to take it back to its roots".

An education system inter-linked with one cultural heritage on one's hand and economic and scientific development on the other is only viable medium to take one successfully ahead towards the 21st century.

An ideal society s visualised by Gandhiji is a harmonious community based not on cold and cruel competition but on co-operation and mutual respect. In his opinion, a spirit of service, sacrifice, and love for labour will replace the mad rush after power and property. Education is looked upon by Gandhiji as an instrument for the establishment of such an ideal society.

Bertrand Russell (1961) believed that the world could be transformed if the basis of education is knowledge wielded by love. Education plays a key role in the development of any country. In India also much emphasis has been given to the development of education. But, India's most urgent and immediate educational need is to adopt her own early ideals of education to the modern changing conditions.

Aims and Values of Education

From times immemorial, India has occupied a very esteemed position due to her rich heritage and high culture. In the ancient period, the main objective of education was only to achieve Moksha (final perfection of self). To achieve Dharma (righteousness), Artha (material goods), Kama (satisfaction of desires), and Moksha which were considered as the moral virtues in the Indian tradition, was the prime goal in getting educated.

Plato defined education as a training, which leads a person always to hate what he ought to hate and love what he ought to love. The modern western thinkers like Sir John Adams defined education as the preparation of complete living, perfect citizenship, and harmonious development of all the faculties of man.

Education, the broad general terms, can be looked upon as a social institution to promote a certain kind of life that is satisfying to individual in accordance with a preconceived pattern incorporating the cherished ideals and values of the society. In period of crises, it has to act as an agency of social control by fostering the basic values that hold the society together.

The greatest scientist Einstein also argued for an ethical culture in education in the following words:

A positive aspiration and effort for an ethical and moral configuration of our common life is of overriding importance. Here, no science can save us. I believe, indeed, solely the practical and factual in our education has led directly to the important of ethical values.

Almost every education commission report released before and after the independence of India has stressed the need for teaching of values like social, moral, and spiritual. Kothari education commission (1964-66) emphasised the selection of values, which determines the future of the society.

The future of society will depend increasingly upon the type of choices each individual makes. This would naturally depends upon his motivational and sense of values for he might make the choice either with reference entirely to his own personal satisfaction or in a spirit of service to the community and a furthering the common good.

The University Education Commission (1948) stressed the inclusion of spiritual training in education.

"If we exclude spiritual training in our institutions we would be untrue to our whole historical development".

The Mudaliayar Education Commission (1953) confirmed the place of the values in the development of character.

"Religious and moral instruction plays an important role in these growth of character".

If in education the highest standards are to be achieved it should be according to the needs and aspirations of the country and its foundation should necessarily be laid upon his history and culture of the country. Radhakrishnan Committee explained the true sense of culture in its report.

"Universities preserve the culture and civilization of a country. If we want to be called civilised, we should sympathise with the poor, respect women, love peace and independence, and hate tyranny and injustice".

The youth should be oriented and grounded in our culture and values and must have a deep understanding of their religion and also develop an understanding and appreciation of all religions. Sri Prakasa Committee, which was appointed in 1959, stressed the need for proper understanding of various religious principles.

"We must not forget that there are always great philosophies both social and spiritual underlying all religions and it would be better if we knew and understood them".

In the life of majority of Indians, religion is a great motivating force and is intimately bound up with the formation of character and the inculcation of ethical values. Kothari Commission Report, (1966) lays the highest stress on the need for moral and spiritual education.

"We recommend, therefore, that conscious and organised attempts be made for imparting education in social, moral and spiritual values with the help where ever possible of the ethical teaching of the great religious".

We should aim at a humanised development of the society, which is possible only through a sound educational policy. For this purpose we have to civilise the human heart through value education. The University Education Commission (1948) also agree with this.

"Moral and religious instructions do not help in moral improvement. What we need is not the imparting of instruction but the transmitting of vitality. We must civilise the human heart. Education of the emotions and discipline of the will are essential parts of a sound system of education".

In this scientific age, we have gained enough knowledge of our surroundings but we have lacked in the wisdom of life. Our scientific progress in controlling our world has not been matched by corresponding advance in human character and virtues. With the forceful emergence of modern science and technology the long cherished human and spiritual values have suffered a set back. One of the effective tools to revitalise our youth and bring meaning and purpose in life is value education, Jawaharlal Nehru (1959) once said:

"Let us pursue our path to industrial progress with all our strength and vigour and at the same time remember that material riches without tolerance and compassion and wisdom may turn to dust and ashes".

In the promotion of intellectual knowledge, the present educational system is neglecting the physical, emotional, social, moral, spiritual and cultural values, which is not desirable. Much emphasis is being laid upon the Information Technology. Information Technology, being a double-edged weapon, has to be managed carefully for the progress of the country but at the same time preservation of values and culture has to remain our prime concern. Even the scholars and eminent educationalists stressed the necessity of an education which has a combination of scientific and technological knowledge along with proper emphasis on moral, spiritual and cultural values. This is evident from the reports of various commissions of education.

University Education Commission (1948) highlights:

"Contents of education must accept the best of what modern advancement has to offer but without neglecting our cultural heritage from the past".

Kothari Education Commission (1964-66) observes:

"A combination of knowledge and lack of essential values may be dangerous to society".

"If modernisation has to be a living force, it must derive its strength from the strength of the spirit".

National Policy on Education (1986) stresses:

"The pre-occupation with modern technologies cannot be allowed to sever our new generations from the roots in India's history and culture. De-culturisation, de-humanisation and alienation must be avoided at all costs. Education can and must bring about the fine synthesis between change oriented technologies and the country's continuity of cultural tradition".

A good society, whether national or global can only be built on the quality of its individual members who must be wise, compassionate, courageous and creative.

T.N. Seshan, the former Chief Election Commissioner of India (1994), has called for a value-based education in colleges.

"Educational institutions must not be like factories with assembly line for producing graduates. Moral and ethics must be incorporated in the curriculum. Fundamental values like human compassion and willingness to sacrifice must be inculcated in the students".

The greatest challenge before Indian education is to inculcate in the people a scientific temper, an unwavering commitment to the values of national integration, equality, human dignity, and universal brotherhood ignoring all barriers of caste, creed, gender, religion, language and region.

Ahlawat (1991) expressed his views in this context as follows:

"More than mountains of butter and guns we need sound educational arrangements and programmes based on indigenous philosophy so that man through his rational thinking rises above parochialism, factionalism, regionalism and narrow nationalism and creates a society wherein his biological survival is assured and the inner being blooms".

According to International Commission on Education, "the aim of education is to transform a person into a complete man. It results in a perfect integration of physical, emotional, intellectual and spiritual capabilities of a person. We have to realise and put into action the true meaning of education. Right education leads to refinement of conduct. Good intellect alone can lead to happiness in the family, prosperity in the nation and peace in the world".

Therefore, it can be summarised from the earlier presentation on the importance of education which is in the final analysis should promote an integrated and wholesome personality acceptable and productive in the society and nation at large. A value oriented education, highlighting and focussing on the values of life to promote the quality of living becomes a necessity.

Values play a very dominant part motivating and sustaining the active and concrete contribution of a person to himself and to others. This brings us to the necessity to study what the values are, the nature, the scope and functions of values in the life of a person and especially, in the education of a person which more or less determines the quality of the person's contribution and interaction in the community.

The following section, therefore, deals with values and their importance in the educational sphere.

Meaning of Values

Values can be best described through a series of definitions given by distinguished educationalists. In their attempts to define values, that they have very clearly brought about the meaning, the conceptualisation, the scope and ambit of values.

Kluckhohn (1957) defined value as a conception, explicit or implicit distinctive of an individual or characteristic of a group of the desirable, which influences the selection from available modes and ends of action. Kluckhohn emphasised the mode of selection of desirable processes from among the available.

Rokeach (1973) explained value as an enduring belief, a specific mode of conduct or end state existence along a continuum of relative importance.

Pepper (1958) going along the same lines interprets values as a selection process.

"The term values may refer to interests, pleasures, likes, preferences, duties, moral obligations, desires, wants, need, aversions and attractions and many other modalities of selective orientation".

Values are yardstick of beliefs that influence our behaviourism and help in the making of choices. A value can itself be defined as a belief, which guides human behaviour and helps in making decisions about choices. Mascarenhas (1983) further explains:

"A value is an attitude for or against an event or phenomenon based on a belief that it benefits or penalises some individual, group or institution or more simply value is defined as a belief upon which man acts by preferences".

The definition of value is considered to be a measure of human aspirations according to Marganau (1959). He defines values in terms of satisfaction of human wants. The meaning of this saying is that the behaviour of man is motivated by the values. Social acceptance appears to be an important norm for accepting a value. According to Anitha Shetty, (1997) value is the quality of anything that renders it desirable or that which is prized, held in respect, deemed worthy or esteemed. Values may be described as a system of personality traits which are in harmony with the inner nature of an individual and which are in accordance with the values approved by the society.

Chandra Lekha (1995) also supports this view when she explains:

"Values are standards or patterns of choice that guide persons and groups towards satisfaction, fulfillment and meaning"

Here, values serve as the authorities in the name of which choices are made and action is taken.

Muthukumaran (1991) gives a new dimension of the meaning of a value:

"Value is a philosophical concept. The philosophy about value is that value should help any one to seek the real knowledge and goal of life in a righteous manner".

In philosophical context, values are those standards or a code for moral behaviour conditioned by one's cultural tenets and guarded by conscience, according to which human being is supposed to conduct himself and shape his life pattern by integrating his beliefs, ideas and attitudes to realise cherished ideals and aims of life.

A value attains three levels of manifestations as a professed value of what we believe in, an operational value of what we practice and a dynamic value of what we learn from our experiences.

From the foregoing definitions, it can be deduced that a value is an enduring belief, which guides our actions, our attitudes and our judgements beyond immediate goals to more ultimate goals. It is believed that a person shapes himself through his choices of values and brings form and life to his being. A value becomes a person's idea of what is desirable, what he and others want, and not necessarily what he actually wants.

Value Education

Education, in other words, must initiate a life long process of developmental exploration within its two dimensions, one of the self and the second of the community and the wider society. This emphasises the need for value education.

Though India is a land of rich cultural and spiritual heritage, a look at the current scenario poses a number of challenges. It is becoming clear that several ethical principles of yesteryears such as adherence to truth, nonviolence, respect for elders, commitment to morality etc., are losing their priority. The youth of our country are confronted with disintegrating values. One of the effective tools to revitalise our youth and bring meaning and purpose in life is value education.

India is known for its rich cultural and spiritual heritage and the need for a value system through education has been felt and recognised through the centuries. The Education Commission Reports of independent India have always emphasised the paramount significance of value oriented education and have repeatedly expressed the need of introducing viable courses to meet this end.

Kothari Commission (1964-66) expresses:

"A serious defect in the school system is the absence of provision for education in social, moral and spiritual values. A national system of education that is related to life, needs and aspirations of the people cannot afford to ignore this purposeful force".

National Policy on Education (1986) desires:

"The growing concern over the erosion of essential values and an increasing cynicism in society has brought to focus the need for re-adjustments in the curriculum in order to make education as forceful tool for the cultivation of social and moral values".

Value education, on the other hand, means a positive effort for bringing about a synthesis of physical, intellectual, emotional, aesthetic, moral and spiritual values in a human being T.K.N. Unninathan, (1988) a former vice-chancellor of the University of Rajasthan emphasised the need to inculcate values at all levels of our society without which we will not be in a position to arrest our accelerating social degradation.

Value education leads to personality development and gets reflected in its professional performance of individuals as well as of service institutions and the production processes of the country's economy.

Tabe (1962) expects educators to control the value systems:

"If educators can control the value pattern of the individual, they can control the future of the society".

When we speak of value orientation as integral to the educational process in schools, what we have in mind is to help individuals to develop their behavioural patterns so that they sub-serve the large interests of society besides developing their individual personality and enhancing their career prospects. Value education, as we discuss the problem today, is an attempt to rehabilitate man as an ally of man and the environment in which he can best survive as an enlightened being.

Education at present, with its emphasis on consumerism and competition for achievement, has sidelined its central concern for the full development of the human personality. Value education, which needs to be looked upon as an essential aspect for the overall qualitative improvement of education, is being neglected to a great extent. In this context, many educationalists and statesmen have expressed in the National Education Commission reports the crying need to balance the knowledge and skills which science and technology brings, with the values and insights associated with ethics and religion at its best.

As teachers have always claimed a special capacity to influence conduct and to shape moral character, the society expects them to develop not only knowledge but also ethical values among students thus creating an environment that would foster fraternity amongst mankind. Value education is a joint-enquiry by the teacher and the taught and it provides immense possibilities for dialogical encounter between persons. This encounter helps not only the youth to reflect critically but in the process of learning teaching, the elders who profess a noble philosophy of life are also conscientised to live by the same standard.

All those who are committed to the cause of education need to be concerned about value education. Values combine a person's thoughts, feeling, and actions on a particular belief or issue and establish a harmonious relationship between them. It is this harmony that prevents us from being inhuman and subhuman in a society that is torn and fragmented by various forces and where the loss of treasured values becomes not only a personal loss, but leads to the degeneration and disintegration of society.

National Educational Policy (1986) expressed the same view:

"In our culturally plural society, education should foster universal and eternal values oriented towards the unity and integrity of our people. Such value orientation should help eliminate obscurantism, religious fanaticism, violence, superstition and fatalism".

In the process of learning different curricular subjects one comes to imbibe certain values, habits of thought, qualities of mind that are concomitant to the pursuit of that particular knowledge field. In other words, value education spans the entire learning, cultivation of imagination, strengthening of will and training of character. When we so relate value education to education we can identify the approach as one of integrating values into the very fabric of education.

Classification of Values

Educationists as well as philosophers defined values in different ways and also classified differently using various criteria.

Mascarenhas (1983) categorized values on three levels namely professed values, operational values and dynamic value. The values we publicly hold up are the processed values, the values on which we actually practice are the operational values and what we learn from experiences in order to adopt and renew are the dynamic values.

Many educationists classified values as personal, social and spiritual, although they are not watertight compartments. Personal values consist the qualities with primary reference to the first person singular, social values have a direct bearing on our human togetherness and spiritual values can add a whole new dimension to social and personal values.

Shiela Kaul (1983), Minister of State for Education, Govt. of India observed specific values corresponding to certain human capacities. According to her, corresponding to our physical capacities, there are values of health, strength, plasticity, grace and beauty. Corresponding to our emotional capacities, there are values of courage, heroism, love and harmony. Corresponding to our mental capacities, there are values of clarity, complexity, impartiality and globality.

The psychological correlation between the capacities of personality and other corresponding values is often observed by attempts to derive values and morality from a particular religion.

Anitha Shetty (1997) identified four types of values namely, human, social, cultural and institutional values to be introduced in the educational system.

What is enriching the individual are human values, what is good for the society are social values, what involves the survival of the culture are cultural values, and what include political and moral establishment values are institutional values.

Saroj Bansal (1981) listed out some values which can be sought through the curriculum. They are: Instrumental Vs. Consummatory; Immediate, Vs. Deferred; Cultural Vs. Vocational; Personal Vs. Social; and Child Vs. Adult.

In terms of importance, moral and spiritual values may be classified into three groups namely, trivial, substantial and perennial. Trivial values refer to some sort of importance or significance about certain things, for example the type of clothes one should wear at different occasions. Substantial values are the beliefs which include punctuality, cleanliness, social etiquette etc., Perennial or fundamental values include practice of truthfulness, spirit of patriotism, kindness, towards others etc.

On the basis of the available literature, both in treatises and research a number of values can be identified with their own specific descriptions manifesting themselves in some form or context in the history of humanity. There are values like spiritual, personal, ethical, moral, social, human, cultural, scientific, aesthetic, democratic, secular, literacy, linguistic, humorous, political, economic, national, knowledge and so on.

Broadly, a comprehensive and elegant classification is propounded by the National Educational Policy (1986) of the Government of Indian which classified all these values into three main categories namely Personal Values, Social Values and National Values, which are mutually exclusive and all inclusive. The commission highlights these three as essential and fundamental values for the purpose of education, specially at the school level.

For the purpose of the present investigation, the above three values are considered. The study revolves around the importance of these values in the educational scenario.

It has been identified in the foregoing discussion that the three values, namely Personal, Social and National Values have a major functional role in school education. These three values with their ancillary supporting values are discussed here under:

1. Personal Values

Personal values may be defined as the values which guide an individual towards what is enriching and good for him. These values would be what an individual accepts as ideals, which govern his style of living. These are practiced by the individual alone irrespective of his or her social relationships.

Education should enable a person to refine each domain of his personality and lead to human excellence. Human excellence is reflected in the form of human values, namely righteous conduct at physical, truth at intellectual, peace at emotional, love at psychic, and non-violence at understanding level. Normally, personal values consist in truthfulness, courage, cleanliness, commitment, and such other qualities with primary reference to the first person singular. Personal values can be classified as Moral Values, Spiritual Values, Ethical Values, Aesthetic Values, Knowledge Values and so on. Of these, the moral value is predominantly influential and conditions the other values such as spiritual, ethical and so on. As stressed by Sri Prakasa Committee (1959) on religious and moral instruction, every effort must, therefore, be made to teach students true moral values from the earliest stages of their educational life.

It is the duty of the school to arrange moral education which gives children the skills to develop the power of concentration of mind and the strength of character that can ward off the temptations to which they fall an easy prey. We should feel that moral qualities are of greater value than intellectual gains. According to Mahatma Gandhi, the end of education is character, and knowledge without character is a powerful evil.

So, development of morality is an important factor for the formation of good character. But character building will have to be exemplified in the very lives of the elders. Right effort in which one must exercise will power to succeed, and right awareness by which one must constantly examine one's behaviour and try to understand and remove the cause of misdeeds are concepts that we will have to inculcate in our students.

In the present educational system, provision has been made for supporting education only by giving importance to intellectual growth. But, important moral qualities such as sympathy, co-operation, mercy, commission, love, truth, sincerity, humility, non-violence, honesty, tolerance, peace etc., have been grossly ignored. The development of such moral virtues along with knowledge would be the sole aim of teaching moral values.

Moral education refers to what the school do consciously or unconsciously to help the young think about issues of right and wrong, to desire the social good and to help them behave in an ethical manner. Successful living requires that an attainable goal be identified. Only a healthy personality will be able to do this. Here is where moral values becomes absolutely necessary.

These values cannot be strictly taught in a formal manner in the classrooms but they are learnt by students through the curriculum, textbooks, lessons, examples, demonstrations, and environmental interactions. There is no dearth of such examples in our country where people sacrificed their lives for the sake of nation and in service of humanity. We have to teach our students about the lives of those personalities who established the supremacy in morality and character. Moral values can be, incidentally, and deliberately taught through literature and students may be allowed to discuss the conduct of certain moral characters in the literature to which they are exposed.

Hence, moral values attain an important place in the scheme of education.

2. Social Values

Social values can be defined as the ideals, which the society expect its members to observe in their day today life. Values which decide what is good for the society are often taken as social values. They discuss the basis of the relationship of an individual with other people.

Chitty Babu (1989), Vice Chancellor of Anna Malai University, states:

"The social values in given social context have general acceptability, these values are valued as norms or ideals, these are sanctified and advocated by religious beliefs and upheld by the legislation's of the state".

The major agents of socialisation are the family, the school, peers, and the mass media. The offer themes for reflection on the socialisation process. It is true that educational institutions, educational content, educational techniques are conditioned by the nature and state of development of the society of which they are parts. Kothari Commission (1964) reminded the duty of education for the cause of social integration.

"It was the responsibility of the educational system to bring different classes and groups together and thus promote the emergence of an egalitarian and integrated society".

If the society changes its values system and nurtures its steadfast the educational system would support and rationalise the new changes. At present, our goals of secularism, social justice, social awareness, and professional ethics have come under enormous strain. The youth of today and tomorrow should be imbued with a strong commitment to social values. Integrity, service mindedness, acceptance of other religions, consideration for others, benevolence, conformity, loyalty, and justice are considered as social values for the present society.

So, it is clear that from among cultural, literary, scientific and secular values which come under social values, secular values would need much more focus and ample attention for the present generation.

Being a secular state, India guarantees individual and corporate freedom of religion, is not constitutionally connected to a particular religion nor does it seek either to promote or interfere with any religion and deals with the individual as a citizen irrespective of his religion. Dr. S. Radhakrishnan (1948) has attempted to give an Indian meaning to the term Secularism.

"Secularism does not mean irreligion or atheism. It lays stress on the universality of spiritual values which may be attained by a variety of ways".

It is real challenge to the secularism of the Indian society which is tradition bound, to change the attitudes of people towards religion and public life. So a secular system of education is generally considered to be necessary in our society which is multi-racial, multi-linguistic, and multi-religious. It is thought that this is the basis on which a just, free and open society can be organised. It is also necessary to supplement it by a system of positive values.

Therefore, it can be summarised that the five most essential educational objectives of Secularism are: (1) Respect for all religious, (2) Tolerance of other's beliefs and views, (3) Freedom from fanaticism and narrowness of outlook, (4) Promotion of a rational and objective frame of mind, and (5) Duty to self and society in a spirit of harmony and well-being.

Therefore, education should emphasise the basic unity of all religions, the necessity of following the ethical code preached commonly by all religions, and the practical steps for communal harmony, mutual cooperation, and religious toleration. In the field of education, a secular outlook helps the individual to free his mind from out-moded tradition and makes him receptive to changing and dynamic ideas. It encourages a reasoned and pragmatic approach to conflict situations Kothari Commission (1964) suggested some curricular aspects to be included in the syllabus for this purpose.

"We suggest a syllabus giving well chosen information about each of the major religions should be included as a part of the course in schools and colleges. It should highlight the fundamental similarities in the great religions of the world and the emphasis they place on the cultivation of certain broadly comparable moral and spiritual values".

Along with these features the student may also be given the information that balances this on the other side, namely the illumination that has come from modern knowledge, the concept of a welfare state and of socialism, and the vitalised study of science with its emphasis on open mindedness, tolerance and objectivity.

Hence, it is considered as an important aspect of study in the present investigation.

3. National Values

The values which involve the survival of the nation are national values and the practice of such values is very essential for the growth and survival of any nation. The first element of right living is to serve the nation, the society, the family, and self, in that order. Dedicated and noble personality alone can polish an individual to a state of true culture and right discipline.

India is now facing challenges of globalisation, rapid industrialisation and dominance of developed world which continue to disturb the balance of different systems, namely political, social, economical and technological. So it observed that inequalities are getting compounded at different levels. Deprivation of women, regionalism, communalism, and casteism are of grave concern for the survival of integrated India.

Therefore, the basic system of our education will have to be such that qualities of service, dedication, and patriotism are included in our youth through a totally different pattern of education. Education should give us not only elements of general knowledge but also impart to us that bent of mind, that attitude of reason, that spirit of democracy which will make us responsible citizens of our country. An educated person should be aware of his obligations than privileges, and more of duties than rights.

The preamble to our constitution clearly indicated the broad outlines of our National Values: Justice, social, economic and political; liberty of thought, expression, belief, faith and worship, equality of status and opportunity and to promote among all, fraternity assuring the dignity of the individual and the unity of the nation.

It has been more than half a century since when India has become a democratic government. It is observed by many a political scientists that our present governmental systems do not practice democratic values. India at present is undergoing a lot of trauma and under the present circumstances, the students of this country are required to develop patriotism, and they need to learn to respect, love and protect our country and its lofty ideals. So, democratic value is the value which has to be given more priority amongst all the other national values.

Since India has decided to make itself a democratic republic, the citizens have to be trained to uphold and practice the values of the democratic social order. This can be possible only when the qualities of discipline, tolerance, patriotism, cooperation, equality in thought, speech and writing and the essence of the world citizenship are included and developed in the students. University education commission (1948) in its report reminds the duties of universities in this context.

"We are engaged in a quest for democracy through the realisation of justice, freedom, equality, and fraternity. Hence, it is necessary that our universities should be the emblems and protectors of these ideals".

A democracy cannot be content with a political form but it must acquire an economic content and social passion. Education should help the learner to understand the functions of the democratic state without touching upon issues, which are considered to be political. We should mean democracy as the freedom of the individual to grow towards his self-perfection by means of self-determination. Democratic education, however, is a life long process operating from the cradle to the grave, besides being life wide as well, operating in home, street, school and almost every social organisation.

Tolerance and integration are fundamental and basic values of democratic order. Children have to be taught extensively about National Integration because the problem of national integration is essentially one of harmonising various differences, of enabling different elements of population, to live peacefully and cooperatively, to utilize their varied gifts for the enrichment of the national life. Explicit commitment to social justice and self-restraint become very necessary to combat inequalities and preserve democracy.

There is a lot of diversity in India in respect of language, customs, habits, religion, profession, tradition, and culture. In spite of the marked diversities, there is a general feeling of Indian-ness which transcends all these distinctions. This feeling can be developed in students through education, which has democratic values like equality, participation, harmony, and corporate building up of the nation.

Sources of Value Education

Values are obtained or inculcated through certain informal, non-formal and formal sources. The values identified for a systematic study in this investigation namely, the moral, the secular and the national values are initiated and promoted through some agencies like the family, the society, and in the final analysis the school through the instrumentalities of teacher and the curriculum.

Home: In a way, home is the first school, and the mother, the first teacher. The family influence of the parents, siblings and other relations become the instructional material. In this situation the child acquires rudiments of certain values like teamwork, adjustment and tolerance, obedience to authority, and family ethics.

As a child grows and enters a large arena of the society, the peer groups, and the social structures influences the value systems of the child to a great extent. During this period of interaction with the society the child learns values like honesty, cooperation, integration, non-violence, peace and respect for others etc.

Though, these two initial influencing sources are significant, the sporadic nature and some times the dilution put the onerous responsibility of inculcating values on the teacher and the school curriculum.

Teacher: In a world of confusion and conflict, we have to help our students to develop right value systems. This necessitates on the part of teachers to use various teaching strategies that facilitate the process of value development. Value education is a joint enquiry by the teacher and the taught and it provides immense possibilities for dialogical encounter between persons. This helps not only the youth to reflect critically, but in this process of learning-teaching the elders who profess a noble philosophy of life are also conscientized to live by the same standard. A good teacher knows that example is more important than instruction and he strives not only to keep the ideals before him but also to embody them progressively and increasingly. The example that we expect from the teacher is not that of mere outward behaviour but that of his inner life, the aims of his pursuits and the sincerity with which he pursues those aims. But the present day teachers at school are found to be more concerned with the curriculum requirements obligations than the inculcation of values. Dr. S. Radhakrishnan (1965) addresses the teachers and exhorts them as follows:

"We live in a society, we derive advantages from that society and if the society is in jeopardy, it is our duty to support that society, to defend that society to the best of our ability consistent with our ideas".

As students, values are affected deeply through relationship with teachers, the latter should embody the values of objectivity, tolerance, openness to criticism, and intellectual curiosity. Teachers should serve as models whose qualities inspire emulation.

Prof. Kireet Joshi (1983) has rightly said that the secret of teaching values is to inspire and kindle the quest among the students by means of one's own example by character and mastery of knowledge. It is by embodying values within ourselves that we can really radiate values to our students.

Teachers are the only torchbearers in the dark who can show the path to the society.

Curriculum: Traditionally, the curriculum was considered as a way for reaching certain goals.

Verma (1971) mentions:

"Curriculum should be conceived as an epitome of the rounded whole of the knowledge and experience of the human race".

According to the best modern educational thought, curriculum dos not mean only the academic subjects traditionally taught to the school but it includes the totality of experiences that a pupil receives through the manifold activities that go on in the school, in the classroom, library, laboratory, workshop, playgrounds and in the numerous informal contacts between teachers and pupils.

Thus, the curriculum is an entire process of decision making about the what, when, how, where, and why of education. While making these decisions, certain points and problems arise which have to be referred to a major referent, i.e. value. Thus values provide the foundation of education. According to Titus (1968), values have a basis in man's nature and the nature of the world in which he lives.

Education is intended to develop individual behaviour in desired directions. The concept of desired and desirability is the value. Therefore, values guide the educational process as a whole. The goal of national development, based on selected values, determines the input by way of the curriculum based on aims, values, skills, attitudes and abilities. So the curriculum changes as the national goals and values changes. Continuous evaluation and modification of the curriculum is based on inherent national cultural values, disciplines and the concept of human progress. A valueless curriculum of education will not develop educated people, but will simply make literates. Thus values are the foundation on which curriculum built and guide the entire process and thereby guide society as a whole.

Curriculum is the best means to implement any policy of education. The policy of value education has been suggested by the Government of India in the National Policy on Education 1986, laying emphasis on value education which has a profound positive content, based on our heritage, national goals, and universal perceptions. Programme of Action NPE (1992) emphasised value education as an integral part of school curriculum and highlighted the values drawn from national goals, universal perception, ethical considerations and character building. It stressed the role of education on combating obscurantism, religious fanaticism, exploitation and injustice as well as the inculcation of values.

Cultural values like respect for the old people, care for the poor and unprivileged, and tolerance need to be identified for standard curriculum all over the country. Value-based inter personal relations, importance of racial and religious harmony and concern for humanity should form the basis for friendship and cooperation amongst the people. Development of a sense of pride in our diversity in terms of religion, language and region needs to be emphasised through the curriculum. It should further incorporate the needs of tribal, rural, urban and all religious groups. The diversity and rich cultural identity should be stressed.

A multi-dimensional strategy is required both in content and conduct of education. The deliveries of education namely, teachers, parents, government, social reformers and politicians have to collectively select and agree upon the contents of education and select an approach suited to the requirement of the rising generation of the future India.

2

Role of Textbooks and Need for the Study

The aims and values of education are clearly presented in detail and comprehensively in the preceding chapter. These aims and values can be realised only when they are reflected in each and every subject discipline that forms part of the school curriculum. The aims of teaching a language here in this connection is the Telugu language, the mother tongue, becomes important and relevant for consideration.

Teaching of Language

Language enables a person to understand the feelings of others and express his inner views. Language is basically a communication media, which can be much more effectively done if it is well known to all and very well in practice. The main aim of teaching mother tongue or any language is to develop the ability to listen, read, write and speak in a better way. The teaching of language is intended at imparting knowledge regarding the content of the matter under study, basic principles of linguistics and grammar. Skill of comprehension, expression, appreciation, application, creativity and many other language skills are rightly developed through the teaching of language only. Teaching of languages develops an interest for good literature, vast reading ability, a more matured mind and broad outlook towards everything. This further aims at inculcating right values and good morals along with setting the thoughts of students in the right path and guide them against the evils prevailing in the society. Many of the educational values like literary values, morale value, political values, social values, scientific values, democratic values, secular values, religious values, cultural values, aesthetic values, humorous values, historical values etc., can be inculcated thoroughly through the teaching of language.

These values are to be realised in the school curriculum through some activities, programs and instructional material, of which text book forms an important factor.

The Role of Textbooks

One of the most frequently used methods of selecting educational materials is that of adopting a textbook and teaching the materials contained in it. Textbooks are books which are designed to present the basic principles or aspects of a given subject for use as the basis of instruction. In fact, they are considered as an entire course of study in print. Kothari Education Commission (1964) stated that the quality and content of textbook should arouse interest among children. It observed:

"A good textbook written by a qualified and competent specialist in the subject and produced with regard to quality of printing, illustrations and general get up stimulates the pupils' interest and helps the teacher considerably in his work".

In the early schools, the textbook was an indispensable tool. It provided serviceable answers to the hard questions of what to teach, of the order in which to teach it and at least in some measure of how to teach it.

Cronbach (1955) points out that the textbook is a textbook by virtue of the principles which control its organisations of subject matter and organised in relation to the discipline.

The essential functions of textbooks is rather to make the knowledge which does exist available to the student in a selected and ordered way. And it is always available unlike the teaching film or a television program it can be returned to, re-read, and studied.

Textbooks change in response to changes in educational purpose and also change as the subject matter of given subject changes.

In one sense, the textbooks are by definition conservative. Indeed, this is true of the school as a social institution, certainly one of its functions is to pass on the past. At the same time the school and the textbook as one of the tools its uses must serve as an agency of change and by so doing helps to shape the future.

Hilton (1969) mentioned the functions of a Textbooks as:

"A good textbook should be authoritative in one sense. Its presentation of subject matter should be reliable, accurate, and true to scholarship".

It is clear that any child must learn a great deal about things he cannot experience directly and one way he can do so is by reading. So the textbook writer and the editor must always bear in mind that the learner apprehends meaning in terms of his experiences. Since any one textbook obviously cannot present all knowledge of its subject, it is selective. Being addressed to immature learners, the subject matter in the textbook is appropriately simplified.

The traditional and today, still the usual way, is to use a textbook as the basis for a given course or subject and plays the central role besides various kinds of supplementary exercises. The contents have to be updated made relevant to the needs of the society and the material taught must be challenging enough to involve and develop the young minds.

No book prescribed as a textbook should contain any passage or statement which might offend the religious or social susceptibilities of any section of the community or might indoctrinate the minds of the young students with particular political or religious ideologies.

Because of the great dependence on textbooks, their selection should be regarded as important as course of study construction itself. In selecting texts, the same criteria should be employed as in selecting the materials of instruction and organising them into courses of study.

At present, there are textbook committees formed by government in different states and these committees review the books submitted to them by publishers and recommended textbooks in the various subjects that might be used by pupils in different grades.

Textbooks in Mother Tongue

Amongst languages, the highest importance is to be given to the mother tongue. It is a most potent and comprehensive medium for the education of the students' entire personality. Mahatma Gandhi says:

"The school must be an extension of home: there must be concordance between the impressions which a child gathers at home and at school—if the best results are to be obtained. Education through the medium of a strange tongue breaks the concordance, which should exist".

Through mother tongue, a good teacher can train his pupils in clear thinking, which is one of the most important objectives of education. Pupils develop self-expression which besides being a great social gift, is an essential quality for successful democratic citizenship through their own language. They can also build up literary appreciation and good taste and educate the emotions through mother tongue.

Education through mother tongue needs to be ensured because it is an important medium for inculcating, fostering and, propagating moral values and national, cultural heritage. It also provides a useful insight into the mind and culture of the past.

Though in the seminars and conferences on "Education for Social Change", the importance of the social sciences to give an orientation to the building up of a new society is highlighted, but the vital role that literature can play in this process is sadly neglected. It becomes evident that great artists can function as conscious and responsible propagandists and the teachers of literature may effectively exploit their writings through textbooks.

As a matter of fact, there has often been attempts to reduce the language and other art subjects with a view to enrich the syllabi with scientific and technological subject course, thereby, reducing even the little humanising components of the syllabi.

No one can say or even think that the minds of young boys and girls can be shaped without imparting in their education excellent pieces of literature and treatises on ethics. Literature is a vehicle for training the character and inculcating the right sense of values through the study of literary masterpieces and communication with the spirit of great writers.

In the task of value formation of students, there are two district steps that have to be taken by an educational institutions. One is making available to the students appropriate reading material, for example, biographics and views of great men who had before them certain values and ideas of life and who practiced them against all odds and making all sacrifices including in some cases even their very life. The second is, personal examples provided by the teachers. The former way will be followed only through the language especially, the mother tongue textbooks.

Radical changes need to be made in the textbook of mother tongue. Along with literary aspects, some new topics must be stressed such as folk tales collected from different regions of India, biographies of all national heroes, human geography of each region, an account of the heritage of each region in arts, industry, and literature and the realities of the social life of people etc.

It is necessary for a multi-religious democratic state to promote a tolerant study of all religious so that its citizens can understand each other better and live amicably together. Language textbook need to inculcate such secular values through its materials as and when an occasion arises.

Concepts of democracy, social justice, equality, national integration, patriotism, universal brotherhood, and international understanding should also be included in the syllabi of textbooks of mother tongue teaching to enable the students and make them as responsible citizens of our country.

Need and Importance of the Study

Education must be a process of libration. In our Indian context, Education is liberation from numerous prejudices based on caste, gender, religion, language, from prejudices based on superstitious beliefs, and form a variety of unfounded fears. Besides, education should facilitate freedom to accept truth and freedom to explore and investigate. Education can be looked upon as a social institution to promote a certain kind of life that is satisfying to individual in accordance with a pre-conceived pattern incorporating the cherished values and ideals of the society. In period of crisis, it has to act as an agency of social control by fostering the basic values that hold the society together.

As a culture of the society is influenced by various factors, due to changes in life style and concepts, a sudden shift in the values is being experienced. The modern communication media offers in very attractive ways all sorts of stimuli and inputs about what to believe, how to behave, what models to follow what type of lifestyle to copy and pose a dilemma to the young person today. After completion of education, young men and women become more self-centred, hanker after personal benefits and do not care about social and moral improvement. It is felt that there is a crisis of character as well as values in human life today.

In order to overcome this sad state, we have to evolve an education system which impart significant values to the younger generations. Values do not help a man in self-evaluation or in self-drive. An educated man without values may generate thoughts, which are harmful. Values are the very roots of human behaviour derived from history, tradition, religion, culture, education, environment and aspiration of the future.

As already discussed that all the definitions of values agree on the point that values influence the behaviour, control, and provide direction to behaviour of an individual. Value has a basis in man's nature and the nature of the world in which he lives and thus value provide the foundation for education. Therefore, all educational philosophies, essentially, stress the values and value-based education.

The need for value education has been greatly stressed by all Education Commissions in the past. The University Education Commission (1948-49), The Mudaliyar Commission on Secondary Education (1953), Sri Prakasa Committee (1959), The Kothari Commission (1964-66), National Policy on Education (1986), and Program of Action, NPE (1992) have repeatedly expressed the need for introducing viable value-oriented courses to meet this end.

It has already been noted that the agencies which help to spread the values are family, society and education, and they all are of equal importance regarding this. The family plays a vital role in the infant stage, whereas the school takes that role during the student stage and the society does its part all through the life. Though, it has been studied that the family, the society and the school pave the way for a student to develop a character with good values, the school has to be given much more prominence than the other two as it is mostly in the school the student gets to mould his character and shape his future.

Children learn values not by learning about them in isolation but through the system of education into which they are integrated and developed. The term, school relates to the world set up of the institution, what it stands for, its policies, the values it upholds, the priorities chosen, the life and example of the staff members, the administrative body, the total school environment, and family most important of all the curricular and co-curricular programs.

Within the education system, it is curriculum that is considered to be the most potent tool in the educators' repertoire to bring out the desired changes. Since the process of education takes place in a society, the basic element in the design of a curriculum must be the social forces operating within the particular social structure. By designing and executing the curriculum for specific social and cultural objectives, the teacher controls and guides the learning experiences of developing human beings. Curriculum is the medium through which we translate social educational philosophies into teaching procedures and the values enshrined in the curriculum stem from the values of society at large. The most powerful tool to convey the respective syllabus in various subjects in curriculum is said to be the 'textbook'.

Textbooks play a vital role in the acquisition of knowledge by students and good textbooks are a necessary to promote thinking and to stimulate originally. The place of textbooks in a schooll education system cannot be underestimated. Textbooks are useful guides in the classroom instruction, particularly for the teachers. One of the most important reasons for using a textbook is to help young pupils gain the power of understanding and interpreting facts and ideas that are presented in written form. They constitute the base from where both the teacher and the pupil may start and continue to work in the process of teaching and learning.

Language and literature hold a significant place in the whole systems of values. From times immemorial, good literature, which may belong to any language of the world, has both nurtured and sustained high ideals and acted as a preserver of the moral and social values of mankind. Through portraying real or fictitious characters and situations literature inspires, encourages and exhorts us to strive for and achieve those goals by adopting a set of values that have stood the best of time. Literature holds mirror to the society and reflects the aspirations, struggles, and achievements of the people. Literature incorporates values which are very valuable and can be profitably utilised by the language teacher. Therefore, language textbooks in mother tongue which promote desirable values for the present society are considered extremely necessary for the school education system.

The social reform movements have led to certain modern social values like democracy, socialism and secularism. Moral values which are mostly traditional have to be continued with the emphasis. So the cultural, literary, scientific, moral secular and democratic values which can be aggregated under the personal, social and national values are considered to be the most important for the present society.

So, the present study is mainly aimed at the realisation of moral, secular and democratic values in the present school level textbooks in mother tongue from standard I to X of Andhra Pradesh. The textbooks of each standard have their syllabus divided into three categories namely prose, poetry, and non-detailed study.

In order to help men and women develop right kind of value systems, the implications of the textual content matter supplied to the future generation is a matter of grave concern. In the Indian setting, most of the children stop their education at the end of secondary stage. Students at this level are at the formative stage. Unless they are grounded in proper values, their future will be bleak and disturbed. It is expected that, when the students at the end of their ten year student career enter the wider arena of life, they must be fully equipped with the right values of life.

Textbooks are analysed in the past, as seen from Review of Literature, in many ways for many purposes. The emphasis of such effort was mainly on issues such as the quality of the textbooks, the enrichment of vocabulary, the portrayal of women in the content and the appreciation of prose and poetry in school children.

There are also studies at the doctoral levels that concentrated their focus on the realization of the values of education in some general literature such as children's literature, literary novels and Sathaka Sahitya poems. But studies which focussed on the very school Textbooks as source of value impartation were not attempted.

Objectives of the Study

The study is based upon the following major objectives:

1.. To examine the extent to which moral, secular and democratic values are being given importance in the current school level textbooks of mother tongue.

2. To study the extent to which these values are being realised in prose lessons.

3. To study the extent to which the poetry lessons are realising these values.

4. To study the extent to which these values are being realised in non-detailed textbook lessons.

5. To examine the content with reference to: *(a)* value manifestations, *(b)* explicit, implicit, and eclectic expression used, *(c)* simple or narrative procedure followed and *(d)* use of contemporary or historical approach.

Scope and Limitations of the Study

1. The present study is limited to the textbooks of mother tongue at primary and secondary levels of Andhra Pradesh which are at present prescribed and used.

2. The values which are taken into account for the present study are moral, secular and democratic which are considered as discussed earlier as most significant and comprehensive.

Explanations of the Important Terms Used

1. *Value:* Values are those standards or a code for moral behaviour conditional by one's cultural and tenets guarded by conscience according to which human being is supposed to conduct himself and shape his life pattern by integrating his beliefs, ideas and attitudes to realise cherished ideals and aims of life.

2. *Value Education:* Value education means a positive effort for bringing about a synthesis of physical, intellectual, emotional, aesthetic, moral and spiritual

values in a human being. Value based education inculcates in students a spirit of service, nationalism, secularism, equality, democracy, scientific temper etc., develops among them a sense of commitment to these values and provide them an opportunity to abide and live by these values.

3. *Moral Values:* According to social learning theory, morality is regarded as internalised control of conduct. Development of morality is an important aspect for the formation of good character. Moral virtues like honesty tolerance, fellow feeling, truthfulness, justice, sincerity, self control, love, peace and compassion which promote good character and direct towards the good and happiness of others are regarded as moral values.

4. *Secular Values:* Secular state is a state which guarantees individual and corporate freedom of religion, deals with the individual as a citizen irrespective of his religion, is not constitutionally connected to a particular religion nor does it seek either to promote or interfere with religion. Values like respect for all religions, tolerance of others' beliefs and opinions, freedom from fanaticism and narrowness of outlooks, promotion of a rational and objective frame of mind and duty to self and society in a spirit of harmony and well being are considered as secular values.

5. *Democratic Values:* Indian democracy is defined as a form of government in which freedom, equality, social justice, fraternity, patriotism, and self respect form the basis. The values which have these qualities and which spread these beliefs can be defined as democratic values.

6. *Mother Tongue Textbooks:* The language Telugu spoken by people in the state of Andhra Pradesh is regarded as the mother tongue, regional language and first language taught in the primary and secondary

schools recognised by the Andhra Pradesh Government. It is also introduced as the medium of instruction in schools and some colleges. The textbook which is used for teaching Telugu is known as Telugu Book or Mother Tongue Textbook.

7. *School Level:* The level of education between the first standard to fifth standard in the schools which have the recognition of the Andhra Pradesh Government is defined as the Primary School level and from 6th standard to 10th standard as Secondary School level. The school level comprises these two stages namely Primary School and Secondary School level.

8. *Explicit and Implicit Expressions:* It can be seen from the textbook content, that the value manifestations projected by the writers are in different degrees and to different extents. In the present study a broad division of values is made into explicit and implicit categories. By explicit it is meant a value concept presented clearly, vividly and directly enabling the student to identify and understand the concept on the face of it. In contrast to this situation, value concepts are also presented implicitly in a situation or a context through a conversation or an anecdote from which the student has to extract a value with some effort, and if need be with the help of the teacher.

9. *Eclectic Expression:* Some incidents or stories which contain a variety of values are presented through implicit and explicit expressions both at the same time to strengthen the context of the subject matter like for example a characteristic analysis of a person highlighting the person's explicit value manifestations like honesty, sincerity, etc., and similar values potential in a conversation, incident and anecdote in the life of a person, in his interactions with people around. Such situations as a whole though they can be split into explicit and implicit categories, are represented as one textbook entry with eclectic considerations.

10. *Simple and Narrative Expressions*: By a simple expressions of a value in the content, it is meant the easily understandable level of the students not handicapped by grammar, style and verbal descriptions. Therefore, the narrative and situation oriented expressions mean a value presented through descriptions, figures of speech and uninhibited style and grammar.

The importance that circumstances the scope and aims of the study is further explained by reviewing literature and research related to the topic of study.

3

Review of Related Literature

As discussed before, the present generation lacks a character which has values, guiding them towards what is good and best. It was also observed that education plays a vital role in the development of values among the people. Hence, the need for value oriented education. Textbooks are said to be the best tools in inculcating the values in education. The necessity for reviewing the previous studies on the importance of values and the role of textbooks, therefore, becomes imperative for further action in this regard.

A review of related literature provides a deeper understanding of the nature, scope, and significance of the study. Review of previous research in any specific area gives the overall picture of the problem. The investigator reviewed related literature and studies done in both abroad and in India to give an insightful understanding of the problem and to find out the gap which can be filled by the present study. Various reports, books, and studies that deal with values are reviewed and their highlights are reported here.

The studies referred to are classified into the following categories depending upon their focus, scope, values analysed and sample material used. The categories are as follows:

Studies on Values in Education in General

Pandya's (1959) study is entitled as 'Measurement of Modern Educational Values from different stand points'. It is limited to an elementary treatment of materials from documentary sources with a view to considering the historical, philosophical, psychological, and practical values in education.

Educational values as the researcher found them were conditioned to time and culture, they were not permanent. In the course of 300 years from the 14th to 17th century different aspects of social efficiency were emphasised at different times and they were cultivated through education. By the end of 19th century, the aspects of morality and viability pertaining to social needs were reflected by the values in education. By the 20th century a set of new values emerged in the recognition of the importance of the school, the students and the teachers.

The existing paradoxical situation in education is attributed by the researcher to the lack of understanding of the comprehensive aspects of the educational values and it is opined that the re-organisation of education with the core values as primary aims would bring again harmony and poise in man's life.

Ahmad (1973) studied 'The Relationship Between Values and Modernity with Special Reference to College Girls'. The main objective of the study was to find out if social changes affected the value system. He selected 400 girls in two phases from various colleges under Patna University and used Annie Point Rating Scale.

The study revealed the following findings:

(i) Fashion mindedness, achievement orientation and, non-conformity were significantly correlated with one another.

(ii) Parental occupation, educational level of the family, and urbanisation effected modernity.

(iii) The study indicated that in spite of the urge to modernise, many traditional values were still operating among college girls.

Reddy (1976) made a study to investigate 'The Role of Education as a Medium of Integration of Value and Effective Value Changes'. The study was conducted on the basis of a questionnaire to find out negative and positive values of education.

The major findings were:

(i) Education which is not significant and real cannot effect value changes.

(ii) The present system of education cannot be considered as relevant to the present needs of society and so cannot be called as ideal.

(iii) Values have to undergo basic changes in their patterns and structures and value conceptions are changeable.

(iv) The present system of education has failed to deliver the real goods because of its innumerable imperfections at every level.

Diwedi (1983) made an investigation into the 'Changing Values and Their Educational Implications'. A Social Value. Inventory was developed by the researcher and the study was conducted on a sample of 400 post-graduate students and 354 guardians of the age group of 40 to 60 years.

The following conclusions were drawn:

(i) The place of residence had a close relationship with religious, ethico-cultural, political and educational values.

(ii) Age group of respondents was significantly related with religious, societal, political, economic, and educational values.

(iii) The old values were not shared by the modern youth.

(iv) Devaluation in the personality, knowledge and character of the political leaders as well as the teachers of the day was revealed.

(v) Students favoured change in the old curriculum of education as, to them, it was useless.

Tarlok Singh (1983) studied 'Educational Values of Illiterate and Literate Adults Belonging to Scheduled and Non-Scheduled Castes'. The researcher conducted an opinion survey and selected a sample of 148 adult subjects from Patiala District on the basis of their level of education and caste.

To study the educational values of the subjects, each individual was presented an auditory cue (word-stimulus). The major findings were:

There existed a relationship between the respondent's level of education and his values higher level of education more pronounced were the educational values.

The illiterate adults considered education comparatively less meaningful than illiterate in achieving the goals of life.

The castes of the respondents did contribute towards inculcating unique value pattern in non-scheduled castes.

Studies on Values of Students

There has been some research done regarding the values of students exclusively.

Kalia (1970) studied 'Ego Ideals and Values of Students' and the study aimed at finding out as to how many of our young men and women are tied up with the old values and ego ideals and to locate the particular segment of the society which has been effected by the modern social change. The study was conducted on a sample of 240 college students of the age group of 16 to 24 years and another sample of 40 persons of the age group 40 years and above.

The study made use of a questionnaire and an Incomplete Sentence Bank (ISB) as a projectivity technique.

It was found that:

(i) A change has occurred in the values and ego ideals of the Indian College students mostly in the peripheral values than the central values.

(ii) The process of modern social change has equally influenced the values and ego ideals of the college students.

(iii) The agencies of social change are education, independence, western culture, industrialisation, desire for higher standard of living, and media of mass communication.

Gaur (1975) has done research on 'The Study of Values and Perceptions of High School Students of the State of Rajasthan and their Relation to Learning'. He took seven per cent of the total 10th standard students of the entire state as a sample.

The major findings of his study were:

(i) On theoretical values, urban girls differed from rural girls.

(ii) On economic values urban boys were significantly higher than urban girls.

(iii) Rural boys and girls did not differ on aesthetic, political and religious values.

(iv) Urban boys and girls, did not differ on social values.

(v) For rural boys none of the values were related significantly to school learning.

Gosh's (1977) study is entitled as 'Distribution of Four Social Values among Certain Strata of Youth and Prediction of Good Citizenship with the Help of Values'. The researcher selected 360 boys and 360 girls of classes X, XI, and First and Second year of B.A./B.Sc., students from various parts of West Bengal. The data were collected with the help of value test and the good citizenship inventory developed by the investigator.

Some of the important findings were:

(i) The increase in the years of schooling had no direct impact on the acquisition of values.

(ii) The youth of the highest socio-economic status had high value scores.

(iii) The four social values could predict the emergence of good citizenship in India.

Patel (1981) made a study on 'The Prevalent Value System of the Students of South Gujarat Studying in Standards X and XI'. The objectives of the study were- to study the philosophical and psychological aspects of value systems, to construct an inventory of value systems and to study the relationship between value system at sex, grade, area and income levels. He selected 21 high schools with 898 students of X and XI standards as his sample.

The major findings were:

(i) As the age increased the students become more sociable.

(ii) The girls scored higher than the boys on rational values.

(iii) In religious values the higher income girl students scored higher than boys students.

(iv) In scientific values, lower income urban students scored higher than the higher income urban students.

(v) Majority of the students appeared to be active in aesthetic activities.

Zaman (1982) also studied 'Social Religious and Moral Values of Students of Class XI and their Relationship with Moral Character Traits and Personality Adjustment'. The investigation was of the survey type and the sample consisted of 560 students of class XI selected from 21 Intermediate colleges of Allahabad District. The tools of the study were the Value Scale and Character Trait Questionnaire, the Personality Adjustment Inventory and a Hindi version of the 16 P.F.

Important findings of the study were:

(i) Among both the urban and rural samples, religious values were the strongest followed by moral values, the social values were the weakest.

(ii) All the three values had the greatest influence on character traits and lowest on personality adjustment.

(iii) It was found that social and moral values influenced the personality traits much more than religious values.

(iv) All the five character traits appeared to be positively and significantly influenced by values. The educational implication of the study is that the development and strengthening of a healthy social, moral and religious value systems among students should be a very important function of the secondary schools which would help in solving problems of student unrest and discipline.

Bhatnagar (1984) studied 'Some Family Characteristics as Related to Secondary School Student Activism Values, Adjustment and School Learning'. The sample of the study included 540 students studying in class XI. The tools used were—A student Activism inventory developed by the investigator, SES scale, Test of Values, Hindi Version of Adjustment Inventory, Students' examination records and questionnaires.

The findings of the study were:

(i) The size of the family effected student activism, adjustment, and values.

(ii) Religious, social and humanistic values were not found to significantly related to the size of the family.

(iii) Birth order was found to be related with activism, adjustment and personal, educational, social and materialistic values, while religious and humanistic values were not found to be related to birth order.

(iv) Socio-economic status was found to be significantly related to activism, educational, and materialistic values.

(v) The broken family was positively related to activism, poor adjustment and high personal and materialistic values while the intact family was positively related to educational and social values.

Paul (1986) made 'A Study on Value Orientations of Adolescent Boys and Girls. The sample consisted of 1076 adolescent boys and girls of Baroda District of Classes XI and XII of higher secondary schools and those of the first year of the degree course. The tools used were the Personal Value Scale, Social Value Scale, Instrumental Value Scale, and Terminal Value Scale, all developed by the investigator.

The major findings of the study were:

(i) The urban adolescents were more highly oriented to competence, maturity and maintaining harmonious relations and strove for the accomplishment of their goal in more mature and competent ways than rural adolescents.

(ii) The college adolescents were more strongly oriented towards applying themselves steadily to goals aimed at more stable and more optimistic whereas school adolescents were more oriented to appreciating the value of tidiness.

(iii) With respect to social values, the college adolescents strove more for social harmony, peace and social service while the school adolescents were more oriented to showing warm affection to others.

(iv) In the case of terminal values, the school adolescents were more strongly oriented towards enjoying happiness and social recognition while college adolescents strived more for freedom and nature appreciation.

(v) The male adolescents were more striving for their ambition and excellence and more service oriented than female adolescents. The female adolescents were more oriented to appreciating tidiness, more aesthetic in nature and conscious of being punctual and regular.

Studies on Religious Values

There are few researches in the area of religion, religious values and religious education. Tandon (1967) studied the attitudes of students towards religion and (Rizvi) (1986) made a research on the study of attitudes towards religious education.

Tandon's (1967) study was based on "The Study of Attitudes towards Religion of Higher Secondary School Students of Uttar Pradesh". This investigation was conducted on a sample of 3,197 students (both boys and girls) of 21 towns of U.P. and the selection was by probability and non-probability sampling techniques. An attitude scale of 50 items, a supplementary questionnaire, Jalota's Group Test of Intelligence and Sexena's Adjustment inventory were all used as tools for the study.

The following were some of the important findings:

(i) Students in general had a favourable attitude towards religion.

(ii) Students from lower income group and girls from all categories showed more favourable attitude towards religion.

(iii) Attitude towards religion had significant positive correlation with all the five values measured, viz., theoretical, economic, aesthetic, political and social.

(iv) Students in general placed preference for political and economic values over the religious value.

(v) Academic achievement had no linear relationship with the attitude towards religion.

Rizvi (1986) measured "Attitudes Towards Religious Education in Relation to Certain Value Orientations". The data were collected from 200 post-graduate students of the Hindu and Muslim communities studying in Aligarh Muslim University with the help of the following instruments.

(i) Likert type attitude scale.

(ii) Rajmanickam's religious attitude scale.

(iii) Kilby's way to live scale and

(iv) Ansari's value orientation scale.

The data were classified with reference to sex, religion and socio-economic status.

The major findings of the study were:

(i) A majority of students held moderate attitudes towards religious education.

(ii) Students of Hindu and Muslim religious groups were found to hold different attitudes towards religious education.

(iii) Favourable attitudes towards religious education were found to be associated with such values as helpfulness, preserving traditions and adaptation to nature.

(iv) Irrespective of the difference in their sex, socio-economic status, and religion, students held similar views with respect to the association between attitudes towards religious education and conservative liberal and scientific fatalistic value dimension.

Studies on Moral Instruction

There were a few studies available in the area of moral instruction. Seetharamu (1974) conducted an experiment on the study of moral instruction and Gopalaiah (1981) made a study on moral judgement in children.

Seetharamu's study is 'An Experimental Study of the Problem of Moral Instruction in Upper-Primary Schools'. He wanted to find the effect of direct moral instruction on the moral development of children. Five hundred and sixty two students studying in standards VI and VII of 4 schools located in different localities of the Mysore District were considered as sample.

Some of the important findings of the study were:

(i) Instruction of honesty and responsibility was more effective for girls than boys.

(ii) Boys improved on non-deceitful behaviour by the moral instruction.

(iii) There was a definite improvement on the sub scale of kindness by moral instruction.

(iv) Scores on the fair play on the democratic character improved significantly for the experimental group otherwise the control group for both boys and girls taken together or separately.

Gopalaiah (1981) made an experimental study of moral judgement in children. Projective tests were used to avoid direct questions; original visual devices were used as projection tests in both individual and group interviews. Sixty boys and sixty girls belonging to 6 different age groups of 7 to 17 years were taken as sample. There were planned to elicit moral judgements like value of life, cheating, stealing and lying. A socio-economic scale was administered and data were collected regarding some items of religious importance along with the personal data sheet.

The main findings of the study were:

(i) Religious background in the home serves as a yardstick to the religious influence.

(ii) Children from higher strata of the society had an interwoven complex of advantages over those from a poor background. It is the child from a low/status background who was tempted to seek to compensate by cheating for the mental disadvantages he so often suffers.

(iii) Moral and ethical studies may be useful in the socialization of the child.

Studies on Democratic Values

There are some studies available regarding the values related to Democracy and Democratic way of life.

Singh's (1960) research intended to study the problems of higher secondary education in the democratic framework. The sample of the study comprised 2,500 students of grades IX, X, XI, and XII and 1,000 teachers of higher secondary schools. A questionnaire was developed and used as a tool for collecting data.

The main objectives of the study were:

(i) Students were very much caste-conscious and only 60 per cent of them regarded India as the home land of all the religious communities.

(ii) 92 per cent of the pupils showed their awareness of a democratic order in the country and 80 per cent of them were in favour of it.

(iii) 45 per cent of the pupils wanted social reform and 38 per cent considered spread of education as the best guarantee for the survival of democracy.

(iv) The majority of teachers were enthusiastic about democracy and 27 per cent thought that the higher secondary schools were preparing youth for democracy.

(v) 85 per cent of the teachers took the cooperation of the students in classroom management.

(vi) 61 per cent of the schools had experimented with self-government by pupils.

(vii) About one third of the pupils complained that their opinion was not taken in classroom administration.

Singh, A.K. (1980) studied the political attitudes of college students and the main aim of the study was to explore socio-psychological concomitants of democratic orientation. A sample consisting of 1000 students (500 boys and 500 girls) belonging to the intermediate to post-graduate classes of Magadha University were selected by adopting the incidental-cum-purposive sampling technique. Singh-Prasad's Religion Scale, Bhatia's Achievement Motivation Test, Sinha Anxiety Scale, Joshi' Test of General Mental Ability and Singh and Das's Democratic Orientation Scale were used.

The major conclusions of the study were:

(i) Highly and low democratic-oriented groups differed on almost all the variables.

(ii) Highly democratic-oriented students belonged to the male sex, middle and low caste groups and lower economic group. They were more intelligent,

achievement motivated, world-minded, intropersistive, impersistive, sociable, responsible and emotionally stable as well as less religious, less extra-punitive and ascendant.

(iii) Low democratic oriented students belonged to the female sex, higher caste groups and the higher income group. They possessed lower intelligence, achievement motivation, intropunitiveness, impersistiveness, sociability, responsibility and emotional stability and ascendancy. They were more religion oriented.

Studies on Measurement of Educational Values

In the Nagarjuna University, three researches were done on the educational values in Telugu Literature.

Prabhavathy (1994) analysed 'Educational Values in Children's Literature. The sample included books on children literature which were directly published, and various related stories published in magazines, papers etc., which were nearly 4000 stories in all. The researcher categorised the entire educational values into six groups namely social, scientific, moral and ethical, historical, entertainment, and language and literary values.

The observations revealed that:

1. Child literature was not being given much importance as it deserves in India.
2. Children were not being encouraged by their parents and teachers.

Sathyavathy (1995) made 'A Study of Educational Values in Telugu Novels'. The sample consisted of Nine novels representing the four eras of Telegu literature. The researcher categorised the educational values into four groups namely social, ethical, cultural, and moral values and analysed the level up to which these values were presented in those novels.

Sai Leela's (1996) study was based on 'Realisation of Educational, Social, Moral, Cultural and Spiritual Values in

Ancient Telugu Satakas'. The sample consisted of poems from Sumathi, Vemana and Bhaskara Satakas and poems from Subhashitha Ratnavali. The researcher observed that all the Satakas which were selected filled with rich values.

So far, the related researches that were considered belong to the studies of value systems and educational values. As the present research is based on certain values present in the textbooks, the need for a review on the research done in the field of textbooks is inevitable.

Studies on Values in Textbooks

School textbooks have commended a great deal of attention in the years just past on the part of the general and government agencies as well as educators. All that attention to textbooks has been natural indeed inevitable because during these years education become one of the great national concerns.

Though there are so many studies regarding the basic vocabulary of school children only two studies have been considered.

Chandrasekharaiah (1964) made 'An Investigation into the Basic Vocabulary of Elementary School Children of Standards I to VI of Mysore State. The objective of the study was to prepare a comprehensive basic graded vocabulary of about 4000 to 5000 words which could be understood by children in all parts of the state. Two hundred primary school teachers (male and female) from urban, rural and slum areas were selected for judging the selection and grade placement of words in the preliminary list. They included 10 teachers from each of the 20 districts in the state.

After the analysis of grade placement of the words, 5000 words were selected to prepare the comprehensive basic graded vocabulary. The allocation of the words in each standard was as follows:

Standards I, II and III 700 words each, standard IV—750 words, Standard V-800 words, and standard VI-650 words.

Kathardekar (1982) studied "Basic Vocabulary of Students Studying in Standard VII". The main objectives of the study was to find out and recommended basic recognition and reproduction vocabularies of pupils of class VII whose mother tongue is Marathi. 300 students from 25 schools were considered as sample and sources of data were textbooks prescribed for class VI by Maharashtra Government and the magazines read by children. Tests for recognition vocabulary were developed by the investigator and for reproductive vocabulary children were asked to write compositions on various selected subjects.

Studies on Evaluation of Textbooks

Pinge (1972) made a research on 'A Critical Evaluation of Marathi Text Book for Standard V'. The main objective of the study was to analyse the mother tongue textbook with a view to find out whether it helped in achieving the objectives of language teaching mentioned in syllabus. An opinion survey was done by taking the opinions of teachers, parents and experts. Data were collected by 3 main questionnaires and additional data through personal interviews with teachers and experts. Additional evidences were collected by interviewing 5 teachers and 5 experts.

Major findings of the study was:

In general, textbook was helpful in achieving the objectives of teaching mother tongue, however, it had some drawbacks, namely lack of lessons helpful for developing patriotism and inclusion of few lessons on blind faith.

Chaudhari's (1977) study was "A Critical Evaluation of School Textbook Improvement Programmes in India". The main objectives of the study were to assess the nature and extent of improvement in textbooks and to reveal the difficulties in the way of textbook improvement. Sources of the study were reports of various commissions and committees set up by both central and state governments, reports of textbooks nationalisation agencies in state. Textbooks of NCERT and NBST and private publishers etc., were considered for the historical method, and for survey method. The sample textbooks included both nationalised and non nationalised books.

Important findings of the research were:

(i) The existing tools and techniques of textbooks evaluation were selection oriented and not improvement oriented.

(ii) There were deficiencies in the aspects of textbook content, language organisation, presentation, illustrations, exercises etc.

(iii) There were many errors of serious nature in textbooks.

(iv) Syllabus, objectives, and bibliography were usually absent in nationalised textbooks.

(v) Latest approach in content presentation was perceptible in some books produced by NCERT.

Prasad (1991) submitted a seminar paper in the conference conducted by Telugu Academy in which he stressed the need for developing language and literary values through Telugu Textbooks at degree level. By pointing out certain lessons from those textbooks, the writer found that those lessons pose a threat to the secular values, creativity of the mind etc., the writer further listed certain lessons which might be useful for the students in developing their character.

Studies on Survey of Textbooks

A few people made their researches on the survey of textbooks.

Maharashtra State Bureau of Textbook Production and Curriculum Research (MSBTPCR) (1974) conducted 'State-Wide Survey of Use of Textbooks'. The objectives of the study were:

(i) To find out the percentage of pupils who had textbooks.

(ii) To find out why some pupils did not have textbooks and

(iii) To find out the extent of use of Non-textual produced by the bureau.

The sample consisted of 30 rural and 20 urban schools from each of the 25 districts in Maharashtra including Greater Bombay from where 275 schools were included. In all 7,72,000 children were covered. The survey was limited to textbooks used in classes 1 to 7 in Marathi medium schools. An information schedule was used as a tool for data collection.

Benerji (1980) made a survey on "A study in the Appreciation of Prose and Poetry of Secondary School Children'. The main objectives of the study were:

(i) How far and how the students at the last of secondary schools attained the ability of literary appreciation.

(ii) Whether there was any significant difference in the appreciation of literature between rural and urban pupils.

(iii) Whether there was any environmental effect in the appreciation of literature among pupils of the same sex and of different sexes. Sample consisted of 500 school going pupils both boys and girls forming two groups namely rural and urban equated with respect to intelligence.

Major finding of the study were:

(i) The norm of literary appreciation of pupils was quite satisfactory.

(ii) The environment had strong effect on it.

(iii) Sex did not influence, and

(iv) Urban students were superior to rural in language quality.

Again MSBTPCR (1976) conducted a survey on 'The Position of Women in Schools Textbooks'. The objectives of the study are:

(i) To determine the extent of representation of women in the characters occurring in textbook, in fiction, and mythology in the authorship of lessons and in Biography.

(ii) To analyse the nature of the recreational activities, professionals roles, and character traits of males and females portrayed in textbooks. The study was confined to Marathi textbooks prescribed for standards I to X in Maharashtra. The procedure adopted was to scan the textbook lesson wise and analyse the content regarding the nature of male and female representation and the analysis was done in respect of eight different aspects.

It was found that references to male situations were significantly more than female situations.

Sarala Kumari (1996) submitted her thesis on "A Study of the Values Related to Women in the Secondary School Telugu textbooks of Andhra Pradesh". The main objectives of the study were:

(i) To study the status and position of women as presented and portrayed in the Telugu textbooks.

(ii) To study the status of Indian women as per the opinion of the teachers.

(iii) To study the relationship between the scores of the teachers based on the content of the textbooks and the opinions expressed by the teachers, as per the opinionnaire on the status of women in society. The researcher used content analysis and normative survey method to collect data. The sample consisted of 250 both and 250 girls of secondary schools, 250 female and 250 male teachers from 3 districts of Andhra Pradesh and VI to X standard Telugu textbooks.

The major findings of the study included:

(i) Though the textbooks are containing traditional and biased attitudes towards women, the teachers and pupils are not carried away by those ideas but have expressed positive attitude towards the positions of women in the society.

(ii) There is a significant difference in the opinions expressed by boys and girls about the status of women.

(iii) The difference in the opinions of men and women teachers towards the position of women in the society is significant.

(iv) There is a correlation between the scores of teachers based on the content of the textbooks and the opinions expressed by the teachers as per the opinionnaire on the status of women in the society.

Studies Abroad

With regard to the printing technology in textbooks Wilson Library Bulletin (1963) reported in the article "New Look in School Books" that most recent text books include pictures of children and adults of all races making up the American people. More over, they picture racially integrated groups. This new policy with respect to illustration was matched by a concern that the contents reflect the pluralistic character of their society and grave full, fair, and balanced treatment to minority groups.

A study of Nineteenth Century Textbooks by Elson (1964) sheds an interesting light on another aspect of textbook change. The study noted that the early textbooks made little, if any, pretense of neutrality with respect to what may be called the traditional values. Rather, authors assumed a moral nature in the universe and sought forthrightly to include values for example, industry and thrift in the learner. Some critics of modern life and education seem to favour a return to such textbooks as models.

Huck (1965) reported that vocabulary controls have been lifted or eased at a considerably earlier level in those published since 1960 and that readers try to reflect the natural language patterns of children for example, contractions are used and there is more use of non-literary selections. He noted that none of the several attempts to develop basal reading programs based on linguistic principles had to that date proved very successful.

Kathan (1971) made a study on "Religious Education in Seventies". He found that the word 'relevance' had emerged in the place of 'involvement' as the theme of that period. A questioning of the direction and social commitments of the churches was sustained by its youth whereas the older generation was careful about personal morals but indifferent to social problems. The new generation saw the ethical priority of the times to be the solution of the problems of the poor, the weak and the racial minorities. Religious education was accused to transmitting largely irrelevant knowledge about the important issues of the day such as racism, poverty, war, drugs, sex, and leisure or student revolution. Curriculum materials and methods reflecting the values of the white suburban middle class were ineffective in reaching the non-white, non-affluent, non-visible of the large urban metropolis.

Greeley and Gockel (1971) have done a research on 'The Religious Effects of Parochial Education on'. Their research was related to the effectiveness of religious schools activity of a student's family, the nature of the relationship between the student and the parents, the type of religious school attended and effectiveness of the school in imparting desired attitudes and knowledge. They found that the primary religious socialisation agent was a supportive family, particularly when there are positive relationships between parents and children, where by children are able to identify with the parents. The family in which both mother and father are supportive of religious observance is a stronger factor than when only one spouse identifies with the religious group. Religious schools are a secondary factor when the home is supportive of the desired outcomes. Religious schools however, are not effective in achieving identified objectives in the absence of the primary support factor.

As printing technology has advanced, the use of graphics illustrations and colour in textbooks has increased. Willows (1978) observed that excessive use of colour and graphics not only make textbooks more expensive but can contribute to inefficient learning. Colour can be distracting as well as confusing to the learner. Placement of pictures in the periphery as well as their size and closeness to the printed word can contribute to destruction and effect children's reading speed and accuracy. In addition, students may be misled to the meaning of a difficult word. He also suggested that pictures should be motivating, should stimulate language, and should otherwise be functional aids to teaching as well as contribute aesthetically.

Solmon (1978) observed that effective instruction depends greatly upon match of materials, teaching style of instructors and cognitive style of students and therefore textbooks should be selected by the teachers who will use them because they know their student population best. In addition, by allowing teachers to make decisions related to choice of textbooks, confidence is implied in their professional competence. The researcher surveyed a sample of teachers and found that 45 per cent of the teachers surveyed by him had no role in choosing textbooks they were required to use. That significant numbers of teachers have no part in selecting textbooks they are to use is related to textbook adoption policies. Implicit in these policies is the need for uniformity in the curriculum and for quality control.

Reynolds (1979) found that MACOS that materials have been attacked most frequent as attempts to spread the religion of secular humanism, which denies the importance of God and a spiritual order. He perceived the decline of local control of education to be the major source of tension resulting in textbook disputes. Although textbook protestors frequently do not insist on what should be taught, they see a mismatch between their system of values and the one set forth in the textbook, consequently, their efforts to prescribe the teaching of certain information or the use of pedagogical method result in subtle if not actual censorship. Their protests also effect publishers by reducing sales of books as evidence when sales of MACOS in 1975 were off 70 per cent from sales in 1974.

Schuhler (1980) showed that the continual development of moral judgement through moral training discussion is dependent on the nature of the group process. Group who had undergone a Maier type group dynamic training communicated in an easier and thematically more concentrated way, and showed greater development of moral judgement maturity.

Higgins (1980) in her review on moral education, also distinguished clearly between curricula of the three mentioned types:

(i) Direct moral dilemma discussion with natural groups.

(ii) Combined moral and deliberate psychological education, and

(iii) Moral discussion programs within regular social studies curricula.

Higgins found the first group to be the most effective.

A review of the above related literature shows that there have been many studies based on values in education. Some studies were based on the change of values between the ancient period and the modern period. The values of people from different backgrounds (economic, social, regional and educational) were also compared and studied. A few researches revealed influence of various forces like family, and surroundings on the values of students. There were also studies, which were done on the attitudes of students towards Religion, Democracy, and Moral Education. A few researchers measured the educational values in some pieces of literature.

The related literature gathered from the studies done abroad revealed that some research was done in the area of textbooks. These included the studies based on printing technology, moral judgement and moral values of students, and effects of religious education. Some studies were done basing on vocabulary, form, and functions of texts. A few studies were done on the role of teachers in the selection of textbooks.

In summary, it can be seen that values have occupied a very primary interest of several researchers. Most of the findings have yielded positive results endorsing the beneficial and developmental role played by values in educational by teachers at different levels of education, informally, formally and scientifically.

In several cases the effort of instruction material in a given curriculum and also the influence of extended reading were found to convey the values directly or indirectly to the students. Most of these studies have concerned themselves with a broad list of values in personal, social, political, religious and scientific domains.

The research method in such document-based studies was, invariably content analysis with a systematic matrix predetermined for the purpose of evaluation.

The present study of the Telugu language textbooks at the primary and secondary levels is a logical extension and application of the procedures, aims, and scope of previous investigations with a calculated difference of evaluating the content of the prescribed school textbooks from standard I to X of Andhra Pradesh in terms of the three most popular and essential values namely Moral, Secular and Democratic.

4

Method of Investigation

Methodology

The present study is "An Evaluation of the Realization" of Moral, Democratic and Secular Values in the Textbook Content in Telugu Language at Primary and Secondary School Levels in Andhra Pradesh.

The nature and scope of the study, therefore demands the application of the popular and approved research method, which is the document analysis. This method has been very widely used by several researchers who have undertaken similar research problems of analysing, classifying and quantifying the written material from a given source into certain pre-determined categories and criterion measures.

In the research reviews reported in the earlier chapters, several attempts have been made by researchers in identifying and locating required evidence on criterion measures. In fact, some of the researchers reported, squarely, based their work on the analysis of textbooks at different levels using the document analysis method.

To name of few, Pinge (1972), Linga Reddy (1987), Prasad (1991), MSBT PCR (1976), and Sarala Kumari (1996) have exclusively used the document analysis method. Prabhavathy (1994), Satyavathy (1995) and Sai Leela (1996) also used the same research method in evaluating some general literature in Telugu language for evaluating certain values of education.

The document analysis by implication calls for a critical, and purposeful analysis of the content material chosen for the purpose of investigation J.W. Best (1992), while emphasising the importance of document or content analysis as an effective, descriptive research method, cautions that the content of the documentary sources cannot be taken always as trustworthy. He recommends that documents should be subjected to internal and external criticism employed, usually in a historical research. But this situation does not exist in the present study as the documents considered are prescribed by the state and are used by the teachers as textbooks in the schools. The author also cautions that content or document analysis should served a useful purpose in yielding information that is helpful in evaluating or explaining social or educational practices. Since there are so many significant areas to be investigated, setting up studies for the pure joy of counting and tabulating has little justification. Therefore, it is stipulated in the present research procedures, not only the frequencies of occurrences of values, but also their nature and quality analysed and studied.

Content analysis is more concerned with the ideas and concepts contained in the content material rather than on the style of presentation. Content analysis is also considered to be a method for a systematic evaluation in terms of both qualitative and quantitative measurements.

As the sources for content material in the present study are the school textbooks, certain specific procedures for the analysis of textbooks need to be mentioned in this connection. Klare (1982) and Dale and Chall (1948), and Fry (1977) analysed textbooks with a view to establish formulas of readability and reading capabilities of the reader. In addition to this primary consideration, the said on searchers have developed check lists that have a bearing on the text book. Analysis relating the content to potentially important aspects such as cultural and sex biases, visual education, and the quality of workmanship. The use of the check list in such studies was further endorsed by Bell (1976). Jevitz and Meints (1979) and Krause (1976) N.C.E.R.T. through the efforts of Rastogi and others (1975) developed a set of principles for the preparation and evaluation of textbooks of mother tongue.

After establishing research method, on the basis of the review of related literature on textbook evaluation and in view of the aims of the present investigation, the following study procedures have been stipulated.

1. Preparation of the values manifestation schedule which details various ancillary contributors in the domain of the main values under consideration, namely:
   - *(a)* Moral
   - *(b)* Secular, and
   - *(c)* Democratic
2. A critical analysis of the textbook material applying the above schedule and quantifying the instances, evidences or occurrences of the value reflections in each of the lessons or chapters in the textbooks.
3. A categorisation of the criterion occurrences standard wise and in the three different forms of the language content presentation namely:
   - *(a)* Prose,
   - *(b)* Poetry, and
   - *(c)* Non-Detailed Form
4. To classify the directness and indirectness of explicit and implicit nature in presenting criterion.
5. Establishment of the extent of the incidence and intensity of the value references by classifying the data into:
   - *(a)* Simple, and
   - *(b)* Narrative and Situation Oriented.

6. A classification of the instances of the induction of the values into chronological contexts, namely:
   (a) Contemporary, and
   (b) Historical.

Value Manifestation Schedule

The value manifestation schedule consists of a list of certain value traits that reflect and contributes to a main value under consideration. The evaluation of the content revolves around the presence and intensity of these aspects in the list. This schedule is by no means, exhaustive.

Table—4.1 **Value manifestation schedule**

Values	**Manifestations**
Moral Values (Personal)	1. Truthfulness
	2. Righteousness
	3. Peace
	4. Non-violence
	5. Love and concern for others
	6. Kindness
	7. Good character
	8. Friendliness
	9. Charity
	10. Honesty
	11. Tolerance
	12. Service mindedness
	13. Sacrifice
	14. Selflessness
	15. Bravery
	16. Self-confidence
Secular Values (Social)	1. Respect for all religions
	2. Tolerance of others' opinions and views (Broadmindedness)
	3. Freedom from fanaticism and narrowness of outlook

(Contd...)

	4. Promotion of a rational and objective frame of mind
	5. Duty to self and society in a spirit of harmony and well-being
Democratic Values (National)	1. Qualities of a good citizen (Citizenship)
	2. Patriotism
	3. Unity and integrity
	4. National integration
	5. Equality of status and opportunity
	6. Freedom of thought, expression, belief, faith and worship
	7. Self respect
	8. Fraternity
	9. Justice-social economic and political
	10. Discipline

Description of Documents

This is mainly an evaluate study of the textbooks in mother tongue i.e., Telugu used in primary and secondary schools of Andhra Pradesh, regarding their emphasis on moral, secular and democratic values. As already discussed mother tongue can be an effective education medium through which values can be developed in the students. As already pointed out the role of mother tongue in developing values is equal to that of any of the subjects in the school curriculum. In primary and secondary stages, Telugu language which is the mother tongue of nearly eight crores of the population is taught as a first language. Along with language learning, vocabulary building and grammar the students are gradually exposed to the literature in Telugu in different forms i.e., prose, poetry and reading material called non-detailed. The material in the non-detailed texts is not dealt on linguistic consideration but only for literary purposes.

The current problem in the state of Andhra Pradesh is that all the textbooks in primary and secondary stages are nationalised i.e., state produced. They are periodically revised by experts through textbook committees formed under the guidance of the State Council of Educational Research and Training. The process of revision of textbooks at present in Andhra Pradesh was taking place from 1992. This has been an ongoing process. Hence, only the documents that are currently in use in schools of Andhra Pradesh are chosen. The documents that are chosen for this study are given standard-wise and stage-wise in Tables—4.1 and 4.2.

Table—4.2 Primary school documents—subject: Telugu (Mother tongue)

S. No.	Standard	Name of the book	Names of the authors	Publishers and year of publication
1.	Standard-1	Telugu Bharathi (First class, text-book)	Kusuma Kumari, B.M. Sarojana B. Rathna Mala, V.	Government of Andhra Pradesh, Hyderabad, 1996
2.	Standard-2	Telugu Bharathi (Second class text-book)	Sarojana, B. Rathna Mala. V.	Government of Andhra Pradesh, Hyderabad, 1997
3.	Standard-3	Telugu Bharathi (3rd class textbook)	A team of teach-ers, lecturers and educational officers	Government of Andhra Pradesh, Hyderabad, 1998.
4.	Standard-4	Telugu Vachakam (4th class textbook)	A team of teach-ers, lecturers and educational officers]	Government of Andhra Pradesh Hyderabad, 1999.
5.	Standard-5	Telugu Vachakam (5th class textbook)	Narayana Rao, S., and Lakshmi Narayana Sharma, K.	Government of Andhra Pradesh Hyderabad, 1994

Table—4.3 Secondary schools documents—Subject: Telugu (Mother tongue)

S. No.	Standard	Name of the book	Name of the authors	Publishers and year of publication
1.	Standard-6	Telugu Vachakam	Chandrasekhara Reddy. D and Komaraiah. A.	Government of Andhra Pradesh, 1994
2.	Standard-6	Telugu Upa Vachakam	Venkata Swami	-do- 1994
3.	Standard-7	Telugu Vachakam	Gopalacharyulu, R.V.V. and Sree Kantayya. V.	-do- 1995
4.	Standard-7	Ani Mutyalu (Telugu Upavachakam)	Karuna Sree B.	-do- 1995
5.	Standard-8	Telugu Vachakam	Jayaramulu, B, and Bhaskaracharya T.V.	-do- 1996
6.	Standard-8	Mani Posalu (Telugu Upavachakam)	Narayana Rao. A.	-do- 1996
7.	Standard-9	Telugu Vachakam	Jaya Lakshmi, D. and Anand Lakshmi C.	-do- 1997
8.	Standard-9	Jaathi Rathnalu (Telugu Upa Vachakam)	Devaki, M.K. and Jaya Ramulu, B.	-do- 1997
9.	Standard-10	Telugu Vachakam	Chandra Sekhara Reddy. D and Samba Murthy. D	-do- 1998
10.	Standard-10	Barrister Paarvateesam (Telugu Upa Vachakam)	Narasimha Sastry. M.	-do- 1998

The findings and conclusions arrived on the basis of the data gathered through the above listed procedures are presented in the next chapter.

An important matter that has to be clarified at this stage is, though the researcher analysed the textbooks in Telegu language the analysis is presented through English language as per the Nagarjuna University regulations. The concepts, the spirit and the scope being important, the investigator found no difficulty in interpreting the Telegu oriented incidents or characters, conversations, illustrations etc., in English. Great care is taken not to allow any distortion in the values manifested through the content of the textbook.

5

Analysis and Interpretation

The present study is "An Evaluation of the Realisation of the Moral, Democratic and Secular Values in the Content of Telugu Language at the Primary and Secondary Levels in Andhra Pradesh".

The research concerns are: The identification of the three values, namely, Moral, Democratic and Secular and their manifestations in the school textbooks of Telugu, the extent to which they are present and the emphasis given to each one of the identified values.

To answer the questions and issues raised in the study a careful and criterion referenced content analysis method was followed using a Value Manifestation Schedule.

Quantitative Interpretation

It has already been clarified in the previous chapter that the analysis of the value manifestation is presented in English language, though the content material is in Telugu, as required in the university regulations. The basic concepts and the value orientations are accurately preserved in so doing.

The first and the foremost concern is to establish the amount of occurrence of the values expressed through a percentage of total lessons in the textbooks as shown level wise and value wise as shown in Table—5.1.

Table—5.1 Percentage emphasis given to the three values in the total lessons

Formula: $\frac{\text{No. of lessons reflecting the value} \times 100}{\text{Total No. of lessons}}$

S. No.	Values	Primary level	Secondary level
1.	Moral values	23	46
2.	Democratic values	18	26
3.	Secular values	5	18

It has been convincingly argued in the earlier chapters which present the theoretical structures of the aims of education, the place of values in education, and the role of textbooks in the exercise are extremely important. In the light of those assertions, and requirements, the present findings represented through Table—5.1 which are 'Prima Face' indications of the quantum of the criterion material, the study is searching for, reflect a sad state of affairs. Obviously, the textbook authors have not made a deliberate attempt to bring in the value oriented references through the content of various lessons. Therefore, primarily it can be concluded that imparting of the three identified values and realising their ancillary manifestations cannot be achieved to the extent the theoretical frame work expects through the teaching of Telugu using the present prescribed textbooks. The main findings of the Table—5.1 are, of the three values, there is more emphasis for moral value and at secondary level an increased emphasis for the same can be seen. Comparatively, there is less emphasis on secular value with almost ineligible emphasis at primary level.

In the following Table, i.e., Table—5.2 the results presented consolidatedly in Table—5.1 were expanded across the ten standards of the primary and secondary levels in order to locate differential value loadings, if any, at different levels of yearly studies.

Table—5.2 Percentage emphasis given to the three values—standard wise

Formula: $\frac{\text{No of lessons reflecting the value in each standard} \times 100}{\text{Total No. of lessons in each standard}}$

Values	Std. 1	Std. 2	Std. 3	Std. 4	Std. 5	Std. 6	Std. 7	Std. 8	Std. 9	Std. 10
Moral values	46	15	16	28	28	65	50	46	38	31
Democratic values	15	15	16	19	24	45	25	29	11	21
Secular values	0	0	4	9	14	35	15	17	15	10

From Table—5.2 it can be observed that out of the three values taken for the study, moral value is identified to have been given nearly half of the total weightage in the standards 1, 6, 7, 8,. In 4th, 5th, 9th and 10th standards, moral value was given one third of the total weightage. In standards 2 and 3 least importance was given to the same value.

Regarding the democratic value, it is very pleasing to note that the lessons of 6th standard have given nearly half of the total weightage, but at the same time, the emphasis is very low at 1st, 2nd, 3rd, and 9th standards.

It is also very sad to note that the textbooks of 1st and 2nd standards have no lessons at all possessing secular values. Only 6th standard is observed to have given one third of the total weightage and the rest only 10 per cent to 20 per cent.

The main findings of this Table—5.2 are given emphasis was not given to the three values in all the standards. While moral value is given the highest importance in standard 1, there is a reduced emphasis at standards 2 and 3. Similarly, at the beginning of secondary stage, i.e., standard 6, there is a sudden spurt in the emphasis given to all the three values.

This type of fluctuations in the emphasis to values leads the investigator to conclude that developing values through language teaching is not properly taken into consideration by authors. The textual content appears to be selected at random.

Qualitative Interpretation

As the sources for content material in the present study are the school textbooks, a critical analysis of the textbook material is carried out applying the value manifestation schedule of the three values which were considered for the study namely moral, democratic and secular. A categorization of the criterion occurrences is done standard wise, and in the three different forms of the language content presentation namely prose, poetry and non detailed forms for the three values respectively.

A classification of the directness and indirectness or explicit and implicit nature in presenting the criterion is made for the three values separately. The extent of the incidence and intensity of the value references of the three values is established by classifying the data into simple and narrative. A classification of the instances of the occurrences of the selected three values is done through chronological contexts, namely, contemporary and historical.

The data, findings, and qualitative interpretation of the study are presented through all the succeeding tables with respect to the three values.

Moral Values

The frequency of occurrences of the manifestations of moral value, the mode of various expressions of that particular value and the emphasis given to the chronological contexts to present the value are tabulated and interpreted through the following 5.3, 5.4, 5.5, 5.6 Tables.

Table—5.3 gives a broad spectrum of occurrence of manifestation of moral value at primary and secondary levels of the school and in the three forms of Telugu content presented through prose, poetry, and non-detailed texts. The non-detailed textbook is introduced only in the secondary school level.

Table—5.3 Manifestation of moral value—frequency of occurrance

	Manifestation	Primary level		Secondary level		
		Prose	Poetry	Prose	Poetry	Non-detailed
1.	Truthfulness	1	1	1	1	1
2.	Righteousness	2	1	6	2	3
3.	Peace	–	3	2	1	1
4.	Non-violence	–	1	5	1	1
5.	Love and concern for others	3	1	5	2	12
6.	Kindness	4	3	4	2	8
7.	Good character	2	6	8	8	14
8.	Friendliness	3	3	3	2	2
9.	Charity	1	1	3	3	5
10.	Honesty	1	–	2	1	5
11.	Tolerance	1	1	1	4	4
12.	Service Mindedness	4	1	4	3	10
13.	Sacrifice	1	2	3	3	4
14.	Selflessness	2	3	10	5	8
15.	Bravery	4	2	2	5	3
16.	Self-confidence	2	2	2	5	7

This non-detailed textbook generally contains stories and essays in prose. Therefore, unlike the detailed prose and poetry selections made predominantly from grammar and literary point of view, where as in the non detailed textbooks, the selections made are such that the value exhortations are higher to the minimisation of literary styles, grammar and language. Hence we find that the non-detailed textbook, predominantly contains moral value manifestations.

The importance is on love and concern for others, developing good character, promotion of service-mindedness, and displaying the virtue of selflessness. These values are in turn, strongly seen in prose and poetry selections at the two levels. It is amazing to note that the primary values of truth, non-violence and tolerance preached as national virtues by the Father of the Nation Mahatma Gandhi, and inculcation of honesty and bravery are not manifested in the content, at all the levels and forms to the extent they should occur. However, kindness, charity, and self-confidence have occupied average levels of presentation.

To illustrate and substantiate the above findings the following instances from the textbooks are detailed here under.

Primary Level

At this level, two prose and six poetry lessons are emphasizing the promotion of good character. Standards of responsible such as not to go near fire, not to cross limits based on certain acceptable levels and not to borrow indiscriminately are mentioned in 1st standard. While introducing the number '2' the writer quotes that behaviour are of two types namely good and bad. Benefits of good behaviours are indicated here.

The lesson, 'Prasa Vakyalu' consists of eight proverbs which stressed the morals such as truthfulness, righteousness, friendliness and good character. Through a conversation between a girl and a goat in the form of a song, it can be understood that the goat got punishment from the queen's guards when it spoiled their garden. The moral it teaches is that one should behave properly.

The lessons 'Subhashitalu' and 'Animuthyalu' which have poems collected from various sonnets possess many morals like evils of excessive pride, benefits of being obedient, service mindedness, good nature, obedience, respect to elders, optimism in life, not to point out other's faults, to be God fearing, etc., which important the qualities of good character.

The characteristic of kindness is also focussed through more number of references at primary level. Need for having kindness is focussed by stating that a lion kills the animals without any mercy. The same idea is expressed in another lesson which teaches that we should be sympathetic to all the creatures living around us. The same aspect is also focussed by the character of 'Unnava Lakshmi Bai' when she stood against animal slaughter.

The duties of 'Bala Seva Snagham' referred to the attitude and heartedness through the services rendered by it. Qualities of kindness, love and concern for others have been focussed by the rhyme 'Upakaram' which tells that one should do good even to his enemies and show kindness towards them through the role of a sparrow when it gave shelter to her enemy the crow, forgetting their previous rivalry.

The characteristics of service mindedness and bravery are also given more emphasis in the lessons at primary level. Both the qualities are focussed in the lesson 'Rajesh Sahasam' through the character of 'Rajesh', a small boy. He was very helpful to the little baby whom he saved at the cost of his own life in a shipwork.

Smt. Lakshmi Bai is shown as a woman with high morals. Her service mindedness and concern for others can be seen through some instances such as her efforts to abolish liquor, establishment of 'Sarada Nikethan' to give shelter for widows and so on.

Through the lesson, 'Bala Seva Sangham' which is in the form of a letter writing, the boy while writing about the duties of their society, makes a note about the productive work they do towards the welfare of the society.

The lesson 'Sahasam' is a true incident about a little girl's bravery who saved her brother's life from a fire accident, scarifying her own safety. A folk tale at 5th standard also expressed the quality of bravery by the role of an old woman who escaped from a tiger with a clever plan and proved the need for the presence of mind.

The aspect of developing the nature of friendliness is observed through some lessons at this level. The incomplete story of animals in 1st standard explained the meaning of true friendship when a rat helped a deer to escape from a trap. The same aspect of friendliness is expressed by the statement that two girls 'Jalaja' and 'Jamuna' never quarrel with each other.

The poetry lesson, 'Nesthalu' which means friends describe the duties of true friends as they have to show the right path, to be helpful in distress, to share love and so on.

The lesson 'Sahakaram' is a story with a good message about the feelings of co-operation and friendliness given by the birds to a farmer by explaining the way in which all the creatures are useful to one another and that they should not be looked down. Poems from 'Subhashithalu' also mentioned the characteristics of true friendship and stressed the duties of friends.

The concept of developing love and concern for others is focussed through more prose lessons than poetry at primary level.

In a folk story in 3rd standard, feeling of love and concern for others can be seen through the role of 'Bhadradu' who decided to go for the rescue of a king and his nature of being service mindedness is also expressed through the instance when he saved the family of a bird from a snake.

The activities of social service taken by Smt. Lakshmi Bai witnessed the presence of feeling of love and concern for others and in the same way, the functions organised by the 'Bala Seva Sangham' also proved the sense of love and concern of the children towards others. The story about a sparrow and a crow also revealed the aspect of love and concern that is shown by the role of a sparrow.

The need for possessing self confidence is also stressed through some references here and there. The story about a fox in a folk tale proved that one should not panic and lose hope when faced with a danger, by narrating the incident where the fox escaped from a trap with a clever plan. A poem from Subhashithalu' explains that one should strengthen his heart by the feeling that anything is possible with self-confidence.

The characteristic of possessing selflessness is emphasized through the lesson 'Kanuvippu'. The role of 'Kondaiah' who killed his duck out of greed and lost his legs as a punishment proved that anything which is done with 'selfish motive may not yield good results.

A rhyme 'Manakosam' says that the whole nature is offering something or the other for the human beings and it is the duty of the people to help each other without any selfish motive. The role of 'Bhadrudu' also emphasizes the need for being selfless through the services he has done. Poems from 'Subhashithalu' directly teach the concept of selflessness at all standards of primary level.

Need for developing the virtue of tolerance is expressed directly in the 1st standard while introducing an alphabet by a sentence which teaches the benefits of being. A poem from 'Subhashithalu' also tells that one should be patient and tolerant in life before reacting to anything.

The importance of having the sacrificial nature is explained in a poem from Subhashithalu by taking a tree as an ideal example as it helps mankind in many ways when alive and even after death.

The manifestation of non-violence is emphasised through a rhyme 'Santhoshaniki Karanam' which is in the form of a conversation between as squirrel and a wolf. The squirrel tells that wolf the true reason for its happiness as it never do harm to others and that causes immense happiness to it. The moral that causing harm to others will snatch our happiness' can be inferred from this poetry lesson.

Regarding the quality of righteousness, the evils of greed and the need for righteous behaviour are explained through the character of 'Dhanayya' who is basically a miser. He did adulteration in his 'ghee' business and got a big punishment as a result for his greed. A proverb from 'Prasa Vakyalu' also stresses the conduct of behaviour as to be righteous.

The characteristic of peace is focussed mainly through poetry lessons. The poetry lesson 'Sadhistham', is a song sung by children who pledge their devotion towards good behaviour. They say that they will be friendly with all, spread the message of peace, and live unitedly which laid emphasis on peace and friendliness besides good character. Poems of 'Subhashithalu' also expressed the same feeling with suitable examples.

Most of the manifestations are directly and unitedly expressed through the poems of 'Subhashithalu', collected from various sonnets. The remaining manifestations such as charity, honesty and truthfulness are also focussed through these poems at different standards of primary level textbooks.

Secondary Level—Prose Lessons

It can be observed from the Table—5.3, that more references are made on the characteristics of selflessness, good character, righteousness, non-violence and love and concern for others through prose lessons in secondary level.

With regard to the development of selfless nature, through the lesson Madam Curie' one can understand that by doing scientific researches, with unselfish motive, one can be very useful for the good living of the people around us. Aspects of selfless nature and service mindedness are very well focussed in this lesson.

In the lesson 'Durasa' which is a story told by a turtle, the fate of a fox is mentioned as it died because of greed.

Need for unselfish nature and self-confidence are stressed by the role of an old man in a folk tale. While giving reply to the king, the old man explained the concepts of cooperation, helping nature, and unselfish attitudes which have prevailed in his olden days. He criticised the selfish attitudes of the people of present generation.

In the lesson 'Bondu Mallelu' an old man died as he had no money for treatment. He took lot of pains in bringing up of a flower garden which belongs to a rich man. Later on the rich man repented for his behaviour and through this small story, the author tried to convince that one should not be selfish and should give due respect and reward to the hard work.

Qualities like hard work, unselfish nature and dedication can be seen through the character of 'Lakshmana Rao' when he prepared to complete the encyclopaedia' even though he has no financial support from any body.

There are more references to promote the concept of character building at this level. In the story of 'Moodu Chepalu' which is about three fishes, the first one listens to elders and escaped from the danger wisely. The second one also has done this a bit lately. But the third fish lost her life because of its disobedience and this story stresses the need for good behaviour.

The lesson 'Lekha' which means a letter, a list of moral qualities are directly quoted by the role of a father. The father, in his reply to his son, writes that students should cultivate service mindedness, helping nature, unity, respect towards elders and not to be greedy and selfish. He also suggests that good literature should be read in order to develop good character.

While mentioning the characteristics of 'Jamalapuram Kesava Rao' the author expressed the good qualities that every person should possess, like honesty, patience, obedience and good character. 'Durasa' is a story told to a rat by a turtle. Morals such as to follow truth always, to help the needy, to forsake pride to possess forgiving nature, and not to be a miser are explained directly which are guidelines to develop good character.

The lesson 'Ambedkar Vyakthithvam' proves the point that by reading the stories about great people one gets to know their qualities and can try to emulate them. He said about himself in the lesson that he did not deceive any body, did not commit any sin, had no bad habits and selfish nature. Characteristics of moral value are well reflected by the personality of Dr. Ambedkar.

The manifestation of non-violence is touched well through many references in prose lessons. The lesson 'Prapancha Santhi' (World Peace) very clearly picturises the harm and loss caused by wars and stresses the urgency to have peace and develop the policy of non-violence amongst all human beings.

Messages about kindness, loving nature, and non-violent nature are conveyed through the roles of animals in a small drama played by the animals themselves. The animals want people to be sympathetic towards both the animals and the trees. They make a rule that human beings should not kill animals and trees for their own benefits.

The lesson 'Thumma Chettu' is an autobiography of a tree which narrates many good qualities that one should possess. The tree tells about its simplicity, unselfish and helping nature, and the sacrifices it does. The tree criticises the violence by people towards trees very convincingly.

While writing about the personality of 'Ambedkar' the writer explained that Dr. Ambedkar believed in the preachings of 'Budha' and followed the path of non-violence.

Developing the virtue of righteousness is emphasised through some references at this level. The editorial written by 'Suravaram Prathapa Reddy' exhibits him as a straight forward man without any hypocrisy. He proclaimed that he did not try to hide realities even if they would hurt somebody, he didn't write negatively about others and he confessed that he followed the path of righteousness.

In the lesson 'Durasa' need for righteous behaviour is directly mentioned by the role of a turtle. In the drama played by animals, the animals requested the mankind to behave righteously. The personality of 'Veeresalingam' and the social reformities performed by him have shown his righteous behaviour all through the lesson.

Developing love and concern for others and showing kindness towards others are focussed through some references in some lessons. In the lesson lekha' a father appreciated his son and his classmates for sending money for the victims of earthquake. The act by which the feeling of love and kindness towards others can be developed.

In a folk tale 'Kavala Pillalu' (twins) the act of elder brother who encountered the demon to rescue a kind and his people proved the feeling of love and concern he had for others. The researches done by 'Madam Curie' for the well-being of mankind emphasises the love and concern she had for people.

Qualities of kindness, love, charity, friendliness, sacrifice, and unselfish nature are focussed well through the roles of an ant and a butterfly in a lesson Cheemathalli Viswasam'. The hospitality of butterfly towards the ant when it is helpless and the ideas expressed by the butterfly about having love and concern for others have focussed the above said manifestations clearly. Necessity to possess love and kind heart are stressed by the roles of animals in a play let.

Manifestation of service mindedness is emphasized through some of the prose lessons. The lesson about 'Kandukuri Veeresalingam', an eminent social reformer, describes his qualities like service mindedness, unselfish nature, kind heart and the lofty ideals he owned. He fought with the society for the uplifting of women. He fought for the abolition of child marriages, education for women, widow marriages etc., all through his life.

The lesson about 'Loui Braille' shows him as a very dedicated, helping, selfless and highly idealistic individual. He made the lives of blind people a lot better by enabling them to read and write using a particular script through the researches he made for over 30 years.

Concept of bravery is also focussed through some references here and there. In a story about a crane and a crab the way in which the little crab got rid of the trap laid by the crane stressed the need for the presence of mind and the bravery shown by the crab is worth appreciating. In the story of 'Kavala Pillalu' also, the younger brother exhibited his bravery and rescued his brother and the other kings from a demon.

In the lesson 'Chenetha Drukpatham' lack of honesty and sincerity are mentioned in the news commentary, which criticises the government for neglecting the food crops and developing the commercial crops for more income. This shows that every one should be truthful and honest.

Even the other remaining manifestations are also mentioned in the above prose lessons.

Secondary Level—Poetry Lessons

More emphasis is laid on the development of good character followed by selfless nature, self-confidence, bravery, and tolerance through the poetry lessons.

The concept of good character is stressed directly by the poems collected from different sonnets in the lessons 'Subhashithalu' at all standards of secondary level. Apart from that, there are also some references made to develop good character. 'Chukkalu' is a lesson taken from modern poetry. While explaining the inner feelings of a person, the poet stressed the point that our desires should be within the limits and our aspirations should also be within our reach.

'Urmila Devi Nidra' is a song, which emphasises the concept of good behaviour. The sacredness of 'Urmila' is revealed through the incident when he stopped her husband thinking that he is an unknown person and she also mentioned about 'Indra' and 'Ravana' who spoiled their lives for fulfilling their evil desires.

In the lesson 'Kanyaka' the girl asked the villagers to protect truth and justice and to be responsible and good-natured in life. It can be understood through the tragic ending she faced that one should always travel on the path of truth and possess a good character which lives longer than any riches.

The poetry lesson 'Dammapadam' has mentioned many behavioural patterns to develop good character such as not to make friendship with bad people, to maintain self-criticism, that bad behaviour will lead to sorrow and not to develop jealous and rivalry etc.

The importance to develop self-confidence is focussed through some poetry lessons. A poem from the lesson 'Chatuvulu' gives out a message that one should not be idle but should always be working hard in life with self-confidence and develop self reliance. In another poetry lesson 'Kanyaka', the girl Kanayaka, by giving a speech to the villagers tried to awaken their spirits and self-confidence. Poems from 'Subhashithalu' directly mention the need and necessity for every individual to posses self-confidence.

Need to emphasise the attitude of selfless nature is focussed through some references. While explaining the inner feelings of a person, the poet tried to develop the nature of selflessness through the poetry lesson 'Chukkalu'.

A poem from 'Subhashithalu' in 6th standard emphasizes the same aspect through beautiful illustrations about trees, clouds and noble personalities which exhibit their unselfish nature.

Through the lesson 'Mathru Hrudayam' the poet focussed the unselfish nature of a little bird caught in a fire accident when it requests its mother to leave the place which is in danger without thinking about its little brothers.

The manifestations of tolerance is emphasised through some references. A poem from 'Subhashitahlu' explained that we should have tolerant attitude to know about certain things, the persons, the good, bad and the real truth. Another poem explains that great people never bother about worldly riches and they show tolerant attitude to the circumstances whatever they face in their lives.

In the poetry lesson 'Prapancha Padulu' the poet teaches that we should develop optimism and tolerant attitude to lead to life peacefully. In another poem from 'Subhashitha Rathnalu" the poet describes the personality of a noble man who sows tolerance towards the difficulties he faced caused by people and moreover he does favours even for such people also.

The virtue of sacrifice is focussed through some references. Through a poem from 'Chatuvulu' the poet gave examples from the lives of great heroes like king 'Sibi' who gave his flesh for the rescue of a pigeon, king 'Karna' who gave his 'Kavacha Kundalalu' to Lord 'Indra', saint 'Dadheechi', who sacrificed his body to become a weapon 'Vajrayudha' and king 'Bali' who gave his life to 'Vamana'.

Another poetry lesson 'Poornamma' has various incidents from which many morals can be derived. The incident where Poonamma's parents marry her to an old man tells that one should not have greed but think about the welfare of the children. Poornamma never showed any hatred towards her parents who ruined her life and thus shows the kind nature she possessed.

The lesson 'Pilupu' is the poetry of 'Thilak' a famous poet in Telugu literature who desired to cultivate the qualities of love, non-violence, sympathy, and humanity among mankind. He was moved by the devastating results of the Second World War and wrote this lesson. He explained in a miserable way about the evil effects of war and pleaded the people for peace and harmony.

The concept of bravery is explained through certain references. The lesson 'Prapancha Padulu' which is taken from modern poetry conveys many morals with good number of illustrations. The poet took the examples from sea, pearl, music, ant, umbrella, candle, scripture, rain, dance and many more to explain the profits of hard work and to develop this aspects of bravery and self confidence.

The lesson 'Mathru Hrudayam' which is a story about birds has an incident where the baby bird consoles its mother to be brave and face the danger with good planning and brave heart. This emphasizes the importance of bravery and self-confidence.

Secondary Level—Non-detailed Texts

It can be observed from the Table—5.3, that the lessons in non-detailed texts possess several moral values when compared with prose and poetry sections.

It is pleasing to note that all the five lessons at standard 6, have witnessed the presence of moral values.

The first lesson 'Vemana and Veerabrahmam' conveys the morals taught by Vemana in the form of sonnets in a very understandable manner. Some of them are to give respect to elders, to love neighbours along with relatives, to have a good heart, to stay away from bad people, and to exercise self-criticism. The next part of the lesson which is about Veerabrahmam tells his views about good conduct. He explained the importance of a mother and advised that people should be given respect by their good behaviour but not by their financial status or by anything. These two personalities of 16th century can be taken even now as ideals by the children.

The second lesson is about 'Tanguturi Prakasam' a great patriot. The role of Prakasam's mother also can be taken as a good example for a self-reliant, hard working, dedicated, confident and self respecting woman. Sri Prakasam is exhibited as a good student for not neglecting the studies even though he was poor and had to undertake several household and occupational tasks. He can also be taken as an example for dedication, hard work, helping nature, bravery, leadership, self-respect and many such good qualities.

The third lesson is about a famous engineer 'Mokshagundam Vishweshwaraiah' who is known for his good qualities. Some of them are his helping nature, hard work and dedication which can be identified through out the lesson. The motto he followed was, work is worship' and the love he showed towards his enemies, his self reliance and self confidence are to be followed for the attainment of good nature.

Mother Teresa was a well known personality all over the world for her loving heart. Her story in the fourth lesson depicts her service mindedness, compassion, selfless character and goodness to the reader. Her readiness to help those in pain and agony, her dedication in her work, her love towards the suffering have to be followed by one and all.

The lesson 'P.T. Usha', and athlete portrays her as an ideal lady with many good qualities. She made her parents proud which is the duty of every child.

Out of 6 non-detailed lessons from the 7th standard 4 lessons are identified to be having moral values.

The first lesson 'Potti Sree Ramulu' is his biography and tells about his achievements and sacrifices. He is known for his bravery, dedication, hard work, sympathetic and unselfish nature. He sacrificed his life for the formation of A.P. State. His life can be taken as a model for many morals.

The second lesson 'Sir C.R. Reddy' explains the character of Reddy as a kind hearted man when he donates half of his salary for the welfare of others. The role of Reddy's father was also introduced as a man with great virtues.

The third lesson is about a well reputed Engineer K.L. Rao was inspired by the life histories of many famous people. This is very idealistic to the students. The incident, where Dr. Rao hates bribery shows his sincerity and honesty.

The fourth lesson 'William Carey' gives out many morals through his biography. Cary's character is shown to be possessing many great morals which can be identified all through the lesson. His determination, hard work, and self-reliance can be seen by the way in which he became a professor. His love, kindness, sympathy, grace and care for the people around him can be understood by various activities he performed which were stated in the lesson.

Regarding 8th standard, three lessons are observed to be having moral values. The first one is about 'Jhansi Lakshmi Bai', a brave warrior. She is well known for her bravery, love sympathy, and able ruling. The various incidents in the lesson show her kind heart which could forgive even her enemies. She had the qualities of a good leader and she could face any kind of problem with a brave heart and never parted from the path of truth and justice.

The second lesson 'Sardar Vallabha Bhai Patel' shows Patel's impartiality, charity, self-confidence, dedication, determination, truthfulness, service mindedness, love and concern for the people through describing various incidents of his life story.

The third lesson is about 'Sir Arthur Cotton', who is known well for his great service he did for the construction of a big barrage. He is shown to be possessing good qualities like service mindedness and dedication. His morals are very high and can be taken as ideals like universal love, helping nature, sympathy and service mindedness.

Three lessons of 9th standard non-detailed textbook are observed to be with moral values. The first lesson is about the great king of Vijayanagaram Sree Krishna Deva Rayalu'. He is well known for the wonderful qualities he possessed. He mentioned the duties of an able king in the book 'Amuktha Malyada' which was written by him. His truthfulness, concern for others, ideal personality, culture, service mindedness can be seen in this lesson.

The second lesson shows 'Sree Sathya Lingam Nayakar' as a great donor who donated all his property which was nearly about 8 lakh rupees to many charitable trusts. His service mindedness, loyalty, simplicity, kindness, and generosity are well explained through so many incidents in the lesson. The very introduction of his character reveals his nigh personality.

The third lesson is about an efficient doctor 'Yallapragada Subba Rao'. Through the character of Dr. Subba Rao, one gets to know that hard work always pays. To protect the whole humanity from the diseases was his main motto. He helped so many poor students by paying their educational fees apart from his free services to the patients.

Regarding 10th standard a part of the famous novel 'Barrister Parvatheesam' is prescribed as a non-detailed textbook which has strikes of comedy in it. In this lesson he travelled all the way to England for higher studies. By his autobiography, one gets to know his unselfish and innocent nature. He criticises people who encourage bribery. Though he faces many insults, he fights all his problems with a brave and confident heart.

Table—5.4 Percentage emphasis given to the explicit and implicit expression of moral value

Formula: $\frac{\text{No. of lessons emphasising the expression} \times 100}{\text{Total No. of lessons emphasizing the value}}$

Level/literary form	Explicit/ direct	Implicit/ indirect	Eclectic expression
Primary level:			
Prose lessons	50	50	–
Poetry lessons	67	33	–
Secondary level:			
Prose lessons	53	47	–
Poetry lessons	53	47	–
Non-detailed Lessons	38	31	31

It can be found from the Table—5.4 that regarding the expression of moral value in the textbooks, there are no reasons to conclude that the authors have preferred one type of expression over the other. This observation is more true regarding the prose lessons. Interestingly, nearly two thirds of the poetry lessons at primary level are explicit, enabling the students to understand the value easily.

Primary Level—Prose Lessons

As seen from Table—5.4, three are exactly equal number of prose lessons with emphasis on moral value which have both explicit and implicit expressions at the primary level.

Among the eight prose lessons with explicit nature, moral qualities like patience, love, kindness, good behaviour, unity, bravery, sacrifice and service mindedness are expressed directly in the lessons.

Regarding the lessons which have implicit expression of moral value, all the lessons are based on stories. Evils of greed have been explained through the characters of Dhanayya and Kondayya in the two lessons namely 'Pisinari Dhanayya' and Kanuvippu'. Helping nature is seen by the role of 'Bhadrudu' in a folk tale called 'Paropakaram' and the need for cooperation is stressed in the lesson 'Sahakaram', through a conversation between Ramayya and an owl. Sense of spontaneity is focussed through two folk stories which are about an old woman and a fox respectively.

In case of poetry lessons, two thirds of the lessons have expressed the moral qualities through an explicit manner while the other one third, through an implicit way.

Primary Level—Poetry Lessons

From among the eight poetry lessons which have explicit expression, five of them are mere collections of moral poems from sonnets which teach morals like obedience, sincerity, hard work, kindness, hospitality, broadmindedness, good character, bravery, compassion, sacrifice, optimism, friendliness etc. All these manifestations of moral value are expressed directly through the poems. The song 'Manakosam' directly quotes some morals such as being helpful to others, living in peaceful co-existence with the nature and so on. The duties of true friends are stated directly in the song 'Nesthalu' and the qualities of good children are also expressed through the song 'Sadhistham'.

The poetry lessons in the implicit category are songs and rhymes with morals hidden in them which are presented through conversations and stories.

Through the song 'Ankela Pata', children get to know the difference between good and bad after some illustrations. The conversation between a small girl and a goat in another song 'Bujji Meka' consists of the moral that one should not be greedy. 'Upakaram' is a rhyme with a story which conveys the message that one should love their enemies and do good to them that hate them which is expressed by the roles of a crow and a sparrow. The lesson 'Santhoshaniki Karanam' explains the true reason of happiness by the conversation between a squirrel and a wolf.

Secondary Level—Prose Lessons

The moral value is shown explicitly and implicitly almost with equal emphasis in prose lessons.

With regard to explicit expressions, qualities of good character are directly quoted by the role of a father in a lesson 'Lekha' and qualities of service mindedness, obedience helping nature and necessity of peace are directly expressed in the lessons of 'Madam Curie', 'Kesava Rao' and 'Prapancha Santhi'. The social reformities taken by 'Veeresalingam', the research done by 'Loui Braille' for blind people, characteristics of 'Pratapa Reddy', need for cooperation and unselfish attitude of old people, determination and dedication of 'Lakshmana Rao', and the personality of 'Ambedkar' are clearly and directly expressing the manifestations of moral value.

It is seen that there are nine prose lessons which are emphasising the moral value with implicit expression. Except the last lesson in 10th standard, all the lessons are story based that convey the messages of morality indirectly.

Need for presence of mind and obedience is conveyed through the story of three fishes and the misery caused by selfishness is picturised in the story of 'Durasa'. Qualities of bravery and truthfulness are presented by two brothers in the story of 'Kavala Pillalu', and helping nature and sympathy are shown by an ant and a butterfly in 'Cheemathalli Viswasam'. Sympathy towards animals and trees is established by animals through 'Adavi Jantuvula Avendana' and love, simplicity, and service mindedness are conveyed through the autobiography of a tree in 'Tumma Chettu', presence of mind and concern for others are shown by birds in 'Konga-Endri', and the result of selfishness is identified in 'Bondu Malleu' and lastly, need for truthfulness is observed in the lesson 'Chenetha Drukpatham', all these qualities are not presented directly but are hidden in the lessons which have to be identified and explained.

Secondary Level—Poetry Lessons

It is interesting to see that almost equal number of poetry lessons are expressing the moral value in both explicit and implicit manners at secondary level.

From among the eight poetry lessons which have explicit expression all the seven lessons are 'Subhashithalu' which are poems which in turn are adopted from different sonnets and the morals that may be directly derived from those poems are to be good, truthful, helpful, courageous, God fearing, service minded, dedicated, patient, graceful, self reliant. Moral qualities related to good behaviour are also directly expressed in the last lesson, 'Dammapadam'.

Unlike the poems which represented explicit expression, all the seven poetry lessons which are emphasising the moral value implicitly have been taken from different backdrops.

The poet gives out the moral that our desires should be within the limits through some good illustrations in the lessons 'Chukkalu'. The lessons 'Poornamma' and 'Kanyaka' are based on the social customs of 18th century which convey the messages of good conduct through the characters of these two girls. The song 'Urmila Devi Nidra', which is based on a mythological story reveals the moral through some illustrations given by Urmila.

The poet conveys several principles of morality with suitable illustrations through his modern poetry in 'Prapancha Padulu'. The evil effects of war and the need for peace are reminded through the poetry of Tilak in 'Pilupu' and the concepts of bravery and presence of mind are expressed by the roles of birds in 'Mathru Hrudayam'.

Non-detailed Texts

It is observed from Table—5.4, that there is an equal distribution of non detailed lessons which have explicit, implicit and eclectic expressions of moral value.

Regarding explicit expression, in the lesson 'Vemana and Veerabrahmam' the two poets expressed their views and ideas directly in a very understandable manner. The services done by 'Mother Teresa' have a direct impact on the minds of the students. The character of Sir C.R. Reddy is also quoted as an ideal character in the lesson directly. The service mindedness of 'William Carey' can be identified all through the lesson. The noble qualities for a king to be possessed are quoted in the lesson 'Andhra Bhojudu' in a clear way. The charitable nature of 'Sathyalingam Nayakar' is presented directly in the lesson.

With regard to the lessons having implicit expression, the manifestations of the moral value possessed by the characters are presented through some illustrations, incidents and events. In the lesson 'P.T. Usha', she is portrayed as an ideal lady with good qualities which can be identified through some events. The truthfulness and ideal nature of K.L. Rao, are shown through some incidents of his life. The life story of 'Jhansi Kakshmi Bai' helps to understand her bravery, love and her efficiency in ruling her empire. Morals like universal love, dedication and kindness can be observed through the services of 'Sir Arthur Cotton'. By reading the autobiography of 'Barrister Parvatheesam' one gets to know his selfless nature, innocence and love for his country.

The last section tells about the lessons which have both explicit and implicit expressions which means eclectic expression of moral value. In the lesson 'Tanguturi Prakasam' the good deeds and ideal nature of Prakasam are explained directly and in some places, the nature of Prakasam is exposed through some incidents of his life indirectly. The morals and good qualities owned by 'Visweswariah' are directly expressed in the lesson at some points and the social services rendered by him are shown by the implicit expression. The ideal and great personality of 'Potti Sreeramulu' is portrayed directly in the lesson and at the same time, the noble sacrifice he made for a separate state reveals his dedication towards his goal in an implicit manner. In the life history of 'Vallabha Bhai Patel' also, there are some instances which have expressed his moral qualities directly and there are some other illustrations which help to understand the standard of his style of living with good characteristics. 'Dr. Subba Rao' also has the qualities of high morals like hard work, dedication, kindness, and service mindedness some of which are expressed directly and some through some behavioural patterns of the person.

Table—5.5 Percentage emphasis given to the simple and narrative expression of moral value

Formula: $\frac{\text{No. of lessons emphasising simple/narrative expression} \times 100}{\text{Total No. of lessons emphasising the value}}$

Level/literary form	Simple expression	Narrative and situation oriented expression	Eclectic expression
Primary level:			
Prose lessons	44	56	–
Poetry lessons	75	25	–
Secondary level:			
Prose lessons	37	63	–
Poetry lessons	47	53	–
Non-detailed Lessons	19	62	19

The emphasis given to the type of expression is equally distributed between simple approach and narrative approach in primary level prose lessons. Interestingly, three fourth of the poetry lessons at primary level use simple approach. But, the same trend is not evident for the content at secondary level.

For prose lessons and non-detailed texts the style used is predominantly narrative and situation oriented. For poetry lessons, equal emphasis is given to simple and narrative expression.

Primary Level—Prose Lessons

With regard to prose lessons which are expressed in a simple way, it can be found that the references made at the first and second standards are in a simple manner and in the form of small sentences. In the 4th standard, the virtue of 'Unnava Lakshmi Bai' are revealed in a simple way. The activities and social services done by the school children are expressed in a simple manner in the lesson 'Bala Seva Sangham'.

With reference to the narrative expression, moral qualities like sacrifice, charity, helping nature, co-operation, courage and presence of mind are conveyed through various characters in the lessons of prose section ranging from 1st standard to 5th and all these references are situation oriented and story based.

Primary Level—Poetry Lessons

As seen from Table—5.5, it can be observed that more poetry lessons are expressing the qualities of moral value through simple approach at primary level. Out of the nine lessons. Five lessons consist poems taken from different sonnets which have expressed the moral characteristics in a simple way. The other four which are in the form of songs also convey the morals like good conduct, helping nature, friendliness and unity in a simple manner.

In case of narrative expression, the three poetry lessons which are based on three moral stories have expressed the morals like helping nature, sacrifice and good behaviour through the story of a goat, through the conversations between a crow and a sparrow and between a spiritual and a wolf.

Secondary Level—Prose Lessons

As seen from the Table—5.5, the number of prose lessons at secondary level that are expressing the moral value in a simple manner are less than those which are explained in a detailed way.

In all the seven lessons regarding simple expression, the activities and services rendered by characters like Kesava Rao, Prathapa Reddy, Lakshmana Rao and Ambedkar are explained in a simple manner. Several morals are directly quoted in the lesson 'Lekha' and the need for peace is also stressed directly in the lesson 'Prapancha Santhi'. The attitudes of Government are also criticised directly in the lesson 'Chenetha Drukpatham'.

The other division namely narrative and situation, oriented approach consists of twelve lessons, out of which half of the lessons have stories with moral values which are expressed through the roles played by birds, animals, and trees. There are two folk tales, three biographies of eminent personalities and one general story with plenty of moral values with situation oriented approach.

Secondary Level—Poetry Lessons

With regard to poetry lessons at secondary level, the number of lessons representing each of these approaches are divided almost equally.

All the seven poetry lessons in the category of simple expression which are all entitled as 'Subhashithalu' are nothing but moral poems collected from sonnets which speak of morals based on facts in a sample manner.

Regarding the other section of narrative approach, there are eight poetry lessons which emphasise the qualities of moral value and which are expressed by narrating some incidents, illustrations, and stories of those concerned lessons like Poornamma, Urmila Devi Nidra, Kanyaka and Mathru Hrudayam. The feelings of poets which emphasise certain morals are expressed in a narrative way in the lessons Chukkalu, Pilupu and Prapancha Padulu.

Non-detailed Texts

As seen from the Table—5.5, it can be observed that more number of non-detailed lessons are expressing the moral value in a narrative manner. Only three lessons have explained the value through simple method and three lessons with an eclectic expression.

The social reforms and moral preachings given by 'Vemana and Veerabrahmam', the characteristics of 'C.R.Reddy' and the ideal behaviour of K.L.Rao are explained very clearly without any prolonged descriptions.

With regard to narrative expression, there are ten non-detailed lessons which have emphasised the moral value through a narrative and situation oriented approach. The life stories, activities, events and real incidents of great and eminent people are presented through these lessons in a descriptive way. The great personalities of 'Tanguturi Prakasam' the freedom fighter, Mokshagundam Visweswaraiah', the great scientist, P.T. Usha', the world famous athlete, 'Potti Sree Ramulu', a noble patriot, 'William Carey', a linguist, Jhansi Lakshmi Bai, another freedom fighter, 'Sathyalingam Nayakar', a philanthropist, 'Dr. Subbarao', a famous personality in medicine, and 'Barrister Parvatheesam' and innocent character have helped to inculcate the qualities of moral value.

In the lessons of 'Mother Teresa', 'Arthur Cotton', and 'Andhra Bhojudu', there are some references which have helped to present the ideal characteristics of these great people in a simple way, and there are also some other references in the same lessons regarding the moral values they possessed which are presented through a narrative and situation oriented approach.

Table—5.6 Percentage emphasis given to the chronological periods in presenting the moral value

Formula: $\frac{\text{No. of lessons emphasising the chronological period} \times 100}{\text{Total No. of lessons emphasising the value}}$

Level/literary form	Contemporary and post independence period	Historical and pre-independence period
Primary level:		
Prose lessons	69	31
Poetry lessons	92	8
Secondary level:		
Prose lessons	47	53
Poetry lessons	60	40
Non-detailed lessons	12	88

The major findings from the Table—5.6 are, the textual content at primary level is predominantly dependent on contemporary situation for presenting the moral value. Both the prose and poetry lessons at primary level utilised the contemporary, and universal situations which reflect the moral value. But, the textual content at secondary level gives equal emphasis to contemporary and historical situations for presenting the moral value. This trend is mainly evident in prose and poetry lessons. But the situation is different regarding the lessons of non-detailed texts where ninety per cent of the total lessons have utilised historical and pre-independence situations to present the moral value.

Primary Level

The prose lessons taken from standard one have the sentences which are used to introduce alphabets and they are found to be very familiar to the children. There are also stories of birds and animals and events like a fire accident, a real incident of bravery and activities of social service done by students which are well known to the children in their day to day life. All these situations are contemporary, universal and being to post independence period which help to emphasise the qualities of moral value.

Regarding the references made in the historical period, five prose lessons represent this period out of which four of them are folk tales which come under historical period and the fifth lesson is about a woman named 'Unnava Lakshmi Bai' who lived in the pre-independence period.

In case of poetry lessons at primary level, only one lesson represents the historical period to emphasize moral value which is a folk song.

From among eleven poetry lessons which represent the contemporary period, six poetry lessons are 'Subhashithalu' with moral poems which are written in the historical age but can be applicable to each and every person at all ages and so represent the universal situation. The other five lessons are songs and rhymes aimed on birds, nature, friends, and animals which are well known to the children and represent the contemporary period.

Secondary Level

It is interesting to note that there are equal number of references made at both the periods to emphasise moral value through prose lessons at secondary level.

Regarding the contemporary period, the lessons are based mainly on animals, birds, fishes, insects, flowers, and trees which can be seen by the students in their every day life. There are also lessons in this category which are focussing the concept of world peace, social service activities and commercial crops and also a story based on selfish nature which reflect the situations of contemporary and post-independence period.

In case of historical and pre-independence period, there are seven prose lessons at secondary level which focussed the biographies of great people who lived in the pre-independence period such as a great scientist 'Madam Curie', freedom fighter 'Keshava Rao', scholar, 'Lakshmana Rao', and another great personality Dr. B.R. Ambedkar who wrote the constitution of India. The other three prose lessons represent the historical period which are based on folk tales like 'Durasa', 'Kavala Pillalu', and 'Kodiguddantha Godhuma Ginja'.

Almost equal number of poetry lessons at secondary level have emphasised the moral value regarding both these periods.

The nine poetry lessons which represent the contemporary period consists of universal morals which may be applicable to any age or period through some of them were written by poets who lived in the historical age.

There are six poetry lessons at historical period out of which three of them belong to mythological period such as 'Chatuvulu', 'Urmila Devi Nidra', and 'Mathru Hrudayam'. The other three represent the pre-independence period which focus the social set up of early 19th century through 'Kanayaka' and 'Poornamma'.

Non-detailed Texts

Table—5.6 indicates that only two lessons from the non detailed texts of 6th standard represent the contemporary period which have focussed the biographics of 'Mother Teresa' and 'P.T. Usha' who belonged to post-independence period.

From among the fourteen lessons which represent the historical period, eleven lessons reflect the biographies of great personalities of India who lived in pre-independence period. The other three lessons emphasised the life stories of Vemana and Veerabrahmam, and Sree Krishna Deva Rayalu of 16th century, and Jhansi Lakshmi Bai who lived in 18th century.

Democratic Values

The frequency of occurrences of the manifestations of Democratic value, the mode of various expressions of that particular value and the emphasis given to the chronological contexts to present the value are tabulated and interpreted through the following 5.7, 5.8, 5.9, and 5.10 Tables.

Table—5.7 Manifestation of democratic value—frequency of occurrance

Manifestation	Primary level		Secondary level		
	Prose	Poetry	Prose	Poetry	Non-detailed
1. Qualities of a good citizen	2	1	3	1	3
2. Patriotism	5	2	4	4	8
3. Unity and integrity	4	2	1	1	2
4. National integration	5	3	2	2	2
5. Equality	3	3	5	3	3
6. Freedom	4	1	5	2	7
7. Self respect	3	1	2	2	4
8. Fraternity	2	2	1	1	2
9. Social justice	2	1	4	3	4
10. Discipline	2	1	1	1	2

As seen from the Table—5.7 the manifestation of democratic value in the textbooks analysed for this investigation shows that the main aspects that are emphasised at the primary level are national integration followed by patriotism, unity and equality. At secondary level, the main focus with reference to democratic value is patriotism, freedom, social justice and equality.

To illustrate and substantiate the above findings, the following instances from the textbooks are detailed here under.

Primary Level

The main aspects that are emphasised through prose and poetry lessons at primary level are explained as follows.

The concept of developing national integration is focussed through many references. The state and national symbols are quited at 2nd class, the explanation of which may evoke the spirit of national integration to some extent. The balled 'Desamanu Preminchumanna' explains the feelings of the poet who says to love the country like our home and to be united. He further tells that all the people should walk hand in hand together forgetting all the disparities for the sake of nation.

National festivals like independence day, Republic day, Gandhi Jayanthi, Teacher's day and Children's day are mentioned in 4th standard which may be helpful to develop the spirit of national integration. The same aspect is stressed in 5th standard through the lesson 'Poola Mala' by explaining the desire and ambition of the people of India to have unity and integrity which will give strength to the nation with the illustration of different flowers in a garland.

A poem from 'Subhashita Rathnalu' explained the concept of national integration with an illustration of a language. It says that though there may be many words in a language which are similar and synonyms the inner meaning is the same. Similarly, though there are many languages in a nation, people are same and use. By describing the personality of "Joshua" also, the writer quotes his desire for national integration.

The need for developing patriotism is emphasised through some references made in the lessons at primary level. The lesson 'August 15' is actually a conversation between a father and his children in which the father explains the freedom struggle and mentions the name of the leaders who led the movement like Mahatma Gandhi, Pandit Nehru, Smt. Sarojini Naidu, Prakasam Pantulu and Pattabhi Seetha Ramaiah and thus evoking the sense of patriotism in his children.

The lesson 'Andhra Kesari' explains the patriotic feelings of Sri Prakasam as he took part in the freedom struggle thereby providing his love for the country and its freedom. His love for his country can also be observed by his forsaking his property and status for the country.

The lesson 'Durga Bai' shows her as a very patriotic lady right from her childhood. This is clearly explained in the context when she gave her bangles spontaneously in response to Gandhiji's voice at the tender age of eleven. She proved her love for the country by joining in the freedom movement using the weapon of non-violence under the leadership of Gandhiji. The life story of Unnava Lakshmi Bai' also proves her love for the nation as she participated in the freedom movement.

Developing the feeling of unity and integrity is also done through mentioning some of the references. The power of unity is rightly explained in the context while introducing an alphabet in 1st standard. By this, one can understand that unity is a good quality and unitedly anything can be won.

The necessity and importance of unity is stressed through the story of a lion and oxen in the lesson 'Aikamathyam'. This lesson proves that even the mightier become helpless when confronted by unity by narrating about the killing of oxen in the hands of the lion when they were separated.

The song 'Kalasi Melasi' proves the strength of unity by pictorial illustration about pigeons who escaped from a danger unitedly. The lesson 'Poola Mala' helps to understand the beauty of unity through an illustration about a garland given by a school teacher who explains the strength of unity to the students.

The concept of equality is emphasized through explaining some references at primary level.

The feeling of equality can be evoked by the sentence which says that all men are one while teaching the number 'One' in the song 'Ankela Pata'.

While writing about 'Joshua' who is a great poet, socialist and a very idealistic person, the writer says that Joshua defied the inequality persisting in the society.

All the poems of the poetry lesson 'Samatha' at 5th standard emphasized the importance of equality. The inter relation between equality and freedom is explained in a very lucid manner. It is said that a country's progress is definitely depending upon the co-existence of these two factors. The poet also said that equality doesn't mean to live in a same manner but to treat all the down trodden equal to self which is quite essential.

The aspects of freedom and independence are well focussed through some of the references made at the primary level. In the lesson 'August 15' which is in the form of a conversation, a boy Murali while conversing with his father gets to know about the importance of 'August 15', the freedom movement, and the real happiness in achieving the independence. The father tells his son that August 15th is a very big festival for the people of India and thus this lesson helps to understand the importance of freedom and independence.

Through the life story of 'Lakshmi Bai' it is very clear that despite being a woman she fought for the independence and achieved her desired in a free manner. The two biographies of 'Prakasam' and 'Durga Bai' also help to understand the truthful desire of both of these national leaders towards the achievement of independence and getting freedom to India.

The importance of developing the concept of fraternity is carried over through some of the references. In one of the poems from the poetry lesson 'Subhashita Rathnalu' the poet emphasizes that concept while saying that fools find difference in people where as the wise treat the whole world as their home and live peacefully.

One of the responsibilities of the scouts is mentioned as developing the feeling of fraternity in the lesson 'Bala Bhatulu'. In the lesson 'Joshua', the writer explained the personality of Joshua in an inspiring manner and called him as an universal man with the sense of fraternity and humanity.

Need for possessing the quality of self respect is emphasized through certain references. Through the lesson 'Mana Panini

Maname Chesukundam' the writer inculcates the concept of dignity of labour and possessing the quality of self-respect by illustrating the life of Gandhiji in 'Sabarmathi Asram'. The writer further emphasizes that we should be self-reliant and should not depend on others to do our work.

The lesson 'Puttina Roju Panduga' is a drama which emphasizes that poor people should be given their wages correctly and should be treated with love and care as we are all one and same.

Developing the qualities of good citizens is emphasized through a few number of references. The lesson 'Bala Bhatulu' describes the aims and ideals of scouts and also their rules and mottoes. By knowing about these things the students understand the rightful duties of the citizens of India.

The first two poems of the poetry lesson 'Sadhistham' have children singing that they will achieve unity, fraternity, harmony patriotism, discipline, service for country's welfare and all such qualities in their lives which are true duties and responsibilities of every citizen of India.

Regarding the concept of social justice, there are a few references focussing the aspect. While explaining the idealistic personality of 'Joshua' the writer said that Joshua defied the inequality persisting in the society. He fought against injustice through his poetry. He shunned any injustice done due to the disparities of religion, caste, creed, genders etc., and he believed in the universal brotherhood and unity among people.

The poems from the lesson, 'Samatha' also emphasise the need for social justice to be implemented among the poor and downtrodden people. 'Puttina Roju Panduga' is a drama with the evils of child labour as the backdrop. It gives a good message in the voice of characters in the drama and emphasises the need for implementation of social justice among the labourers.

Regarding the characteristic of discipline, few references are made to emphasise the inculcation of the habit of discipline among children. Lessons such as 'Bala Bhatulu' which describes the duties and responsibilities of good citizens, and the poetry lesson 'Sadhistam' made few references regarding the disciplinary behaviour. The disciplined life lead by Dr. Radha Krishnan is mentioned in a conversation which may also help to inculcate the aspect of discipline.

Secondary Level

Need for developing the spirit of patriotism has been made through many references at secondary level. The balled 'Samaikya Bharathi' which helps to inculcate the spirit of patriotism was written in the pre-independence period. In this lesson a poem visualises our country, India, as a mother and all the Indians as brothers and sisters. Another poem insists that every citizen of the country should fight like a soldier against any evil to preserve the unity and prosperity of the country. A poem from 'Chatuvulu' which was also written before independence gives a clear picture about the sufferings of Indian people in the hands of the British with a beautiful symbolism which helps to develop the feeling of patriotism among children.

In the lesson 'Sardar Jamalapuram Kesava Rao' patriotism is the main theme. The writer explained the patriotic feelings of Kesava Rao and his participation in the struggle for independence. Kesava Rao did not accept even a single post after independence which shows that a true lover of the country never fights for power or wealth but he does it for his country's glory which is true patriotism.

A poem from the lesson 'Kanksha' has the flower saying that it prefers to lie down on the tombs of the great heroes of the country who fought in the freedom struggle and gave their lives to free Indian from the clutches of slavery. These words stimulate love for the country and also the feeling of patriotism.

'Suravaram Prathapa Reddy' was a fighter who fought with a pen but not with a sword. He evoked patriotism in the Telangana people through his editorials which were more than two thousand (2000) in the 'Golkonda' paper. He fought for the downtrodden people of Telangana who were in the clutches of the Royal Nizams and proved his love for the country.

'Sangam Lakshmi Bai' was a freedom fighter and the government recognised her courage by honouring with a Bronze plate. After knowing about Gandhiji's freedom movements, the patriotism underlying in her soul woke up and she participated in those movements and became one of Gandhiji's disciple.

Developing the feeling of equality is also made through mentioning some references at this level. A poem from the ballad 'Samaikya Bharathi' shows the poet's desire for an equality amongst all the people of the nation. He wants to set a new democracy by making all the people equal and remove the barriers of poor and rich, urban and rural, labour class and high class and so on.

In another lesson 'Mundadugu' the writer conveys his message in the form of a conversation between a brother, a sister and their grand mother. The writer through the character of Hima, the sister, expresses that a country like ours can move towards development only when all the people inhibiting in the country feel one so that all the differences between them are perished. Even the male domination should be stopped and all the people should strive for the growth of the nation as one soul in different bodies.

'Sardar Jamalapuram Kesava Rao', a freedom fighter fought for the rights of the downtrodden people who were being suppressed by the rich people and it can be inferred through his character that even the poor, tribals, and uneducated have to be given their share of what rightfully belongs to them which is true democracy.

'Parabrahmam' is a song written by the famous poet 'Annamayya' who stressed the concept of equality through his writings though he belonged to the 14th century A.D. He sings that god is Omnipresent and there are no differences of castes and wealth before 'Him'. He gave some illustrations which show no distinctions such as the sleep of a king and a servant; the land on which upper caste and lower caste people walk, the pain of hunger for the rich and poor, the wind which carries both good and bad smell, the sun rays which fall on the lion and the dog, and the God almighty who showers his blessings upon all human beings and finally warns the people that there should be no distinction between them regarding anything and live peacefully with the feeling of equality.

In another folk tale from the 9th standard an old man recalls his good olden days and tells the king that during those days there was equality among people and nobody owned the land. All the people used to do farming wherever they pleased and the tiller is the owner of the land which is true socialism.

There are some more references made to develop the feelings of freedom and independence. The writer of the lesson 'Sardar Jamalapuram Kesava Rao' explained the necessity for independence be it either for a person, or for a society or even for a country. The writer quotes that in freedom struggle cowardice should not be allowed and only bravery, determination, and self-confidence helped people to win.

The poet of the lesson 'Kanksha' expresses his views in the voice of a flower. The poet very clearly picturises the inner feelings of the flower by saying that it never wishes to lie on the feet of a king as a gift. The flower shows its disinterestedness in slavery and fortifies that every living being should possess freedom and that slavery should be abandoned.

The character of 'Suravaram Pratapa Reddy' helps to understand the need for independence. His struggle was against the Nizam Nawabs who were crushing the Telangana people under their feet. He was so determined in his task of achieving freedom for the Telanganas that he did not even care for his life.

The poetry lesson 'Sandesam' consists of five poems which convey Gandhiji's message. Through these poems Gadhiji wants to awaken the spirits of Indian and prepare them for the freedom struggle. He illustrates the various freedom struggles of other countries and questions why India should lag behind in spite of its wonderful history.

The need for social justice is stressed through some references at secondary level. The poet of the ballad 'Samaikya Bharathi' emphasises the need for social justice in the country by saying that he wants to establish a society in which the rich and the poor live together and there is no poor being suffered by the rich.

The song 'Parabrahmam' also focussed the concept of social justice wherein the poet 'Annamayya' warns that there should be no distinction between people regarding their profession, wealth and strength and he preached that people should be treated equally as God treats them.

In the poetry lesson 'Kanksha', the poet expressed his views about the need for social justice in the voice of a flower. This can be inferred from the context where the flower tells that it never wants to decorate a rich man's statue who has become rich by tormenting the poor.

The author of the lesson 'Ambedkar Vyakthithvam' mentioned that Dr. B.R. Ambedkar fought all through his life for the uplifting of the downtrodden castes and tribes and also that he wanted to enlighten their lives and bring their lives to a better state of living which shows his concern for social justice.

Need for developing the qualities of good citizens and the duties of the citizens of a country are well explained in some of the lessons. Through the lesson 'Lekha' at 6th standard, the need for teaching about the duties of the citizens right from childhood is very well quoted through the role of a father.

Another lesson 'Lekha' at 8th standard which is actually a requisition letter written by a citizen 'Kaladhar' witnessed the emphasis being laid on bringing awareness about the duties of citizens. The writer shows the right way to bring out the problems into the notice of concerned authorities and enlighten the society to feel the democratic freedom by each and every citizen in a right manner.

The lesson 'Nayakathvam' which means leadership is mainly about the qualities to be possessed by a leader, and makes clear that in a democratic country leaders are chosen according to the rules of constitution and thus develops respect for democracy and good citizenship.

In one of the poems of the lesson 'Sandesam' Gandhiji tells the true qualities of a good citizen namely self-confidence, self-reliance, love for country and so on. He makes it clear that we should not wait for some one to fight for us but fight for ourselves for our rights.

The concept of developing national integration is focussed through some references at this level. One of the poems from 'Samaikya Bharthi' insists that every citizen of the country must and should fight like a soldier against evil to preserve the unity and prosperity of the country.

Through one of the poems from the lesson 'Sandesam', Gandhiji tells that there is going to be a war of justice where in all the Indians should stand united and fight together to free our motherland. He tells them further that united we stand and divided we fall. By this it can be understood that unity is the strength of any nation.

The need for possessing self-respect is focussed through very few references. In the lesson 'Kanyaka' the dictatorship of a king was questioned by a girl. This incident stresses the need for equality of mankind and self-respect to be given for them. The girl Kanyaka warns that wealth and power are not the ultimate goals of any body and tells the people to live with self-respect and dignity.

In the lesson 'Ambedkar Vyakthithvam', the author presented the personality of Ambedkar as a man with high ideals. He respected other also equal to himself and this can be seen in the incident where he stops people from touching his feet. His self-dignity and self-respect can also be understood when he declines to give lectures in a university against his will.

The concept of developing unity and integrity is emphasized by giving some illustrations. In the lesson 'Lekha' the author very correctly writes that children should treat their fellow students as they treat themselves. They should not treat their co-students with respect to their caste, creed, financial status or any such things and they should develop a feeling of oneness.

The lesson 'Chaldularaginchuta' is about Lord Krishna in his childhood days. Lord Krishna goes to gaze cows along with his friends, and there they play together, and in the noon time they all sit together and share their food with all their friends there. By this, it can be understood that Lord Krishna treated all his friends equally with love and affection and there was no rich and poor, caste races, or any other such things in his attitude.

The need for developing the feeling of fraternity is mentioned in a few lesson. The poet of the balled 'Samaikya Bharathi' tells that all the people of the nation should be like brothers and sisters. They should have a feeling of universal brotherhood and they should strive for the country's development in all fields together.

The lesson 'Prapancha Santhi' (world peace) narrates that world peace depends upon the freedom, fraternity and equality of the people and the democratic rule should necessarily be followed for the attainment of world peace.

Need for maintaining the disciplinary life is mentioned in very few lessons. The author of the lesson 'Lekha' emphasises on the discipline of the students through the letter written by a father. The necessity for a disciplined life is explained here.

Non-detailed Texts

As seen from the Table—5.4, it can be noted that nearly half of the total non-detailed lessons are observed to be with democratic values.

Three lessons are emphasizing democratic values at 6th standard out of five lessons.

In the lesson 'Vemana and Veerabrahmam' the writer narrates the biographics of these two great people who almost belonged to the same period of time. Both the social reformers expressed the same views regarding various discriminations between castes, religious, races etc., prevailing in the society and thus inculcated the true spirit of democracy. They fought for a compatible society where all are equal.

Through the biography of 'Tanguturi Prakasam Panthulu' who was a freedom fighter, the writer emphasized the concept of patriotism in a very inspiring manner. The writer quotes an incident where 'Prakasam' proved that self-respect is very essential. The act of his joining in the freedom struggle by giving up his profession shows the desire he had for the freedom of the nation. The life of Prakasam affirms that a true leader in a democratic country should possess higher values, determination, self-confidence and will power.

While writing about 'Mokshagundam Visweswaraiah', a famous engineer, the writer mentioned the qualities of good character, capability, service mindedness and dedication. The writer further writes that the fruits of labour can be obtained with good disciple.

At 7th standard, four non-detailed lessons have emphasised the values of democracy.

The life history of 'Potti Sree Ramulu' comprises many great ideals. He proved that nothing is impossible for a man if he has determination and goals. But the story of Sree Ramulu, the writer tried to develop the feeling of true love towards others and forsaking the regional partialities which may become hurdle for national integration.

Sree Ramulu sacrificed his own life for the formation of a separate Andhra State and proved his loyalty to his mother land.

In the lesson, 'Sir C.R. Reddy', the writer exposed the character of 'Reddy' as an ideal man with impartial personality as he treated all the people equally irrespective of caste, creed and region. The love of his motherland is evident from his own writing 'Musalamma Maranam' which is a true patriotic story and he proved his affection towards the nation through the character of the woman 'Musalamma'.

'Devulapalli Ramanuja Rao' was a very brave fighter who fought with the Nizam government by printing a paper 'Golkonda'. His desire for a free democratic country can be found by various movements lead by him.

The biography of 'K.L. Rao', a famous engineer who won many awards and rewards, is an example for his scholarship as well as service mindedness. He proved himself to be an able administrator through his ideals of democracy.

In case of 8th standard, two non-detailed lessons are emphasizing the democratic values out of 5 lessons.

'Jhansi Lakshmi Bai', the queen of Jhansi, in Maharashtra state, was well known for her prodigious bravery. She fought against British rule courageously and died in a war against them. The writer inculcated certain democratic ideals like self dignity, thirst for freedom and independence, love for mother land, and patriotism through various incidents that were narrated in the lesson.

'Sardar Vallabha Bhai Patel' was by occupation a barrister and as a person, a very determined, courageous, patriotic freedom fighter. He participated in so many freedom movements along with Gandhiji and was arrested many a times for his participation in the freedom struggle. He also fought for the right for freedom on behalf of farmers and strived hard to abolish bonded labour and slavery which are the main concepts of democracy.

Among the total six lessons, only one non-detailed lesson is observed to be with emphasis on democratic value in 9th standard.

The lesson 'Moulana Abul Kalam Azad' is also a biography of a great freedom fighter who also fought along with Gandhiji for independence and even was arrested and was jailed many times. The courage, non-dependent nature, the desire for freedom, impartiality, patriotic feelings, respect for the nation and many such feelings can be felt by his life through the lesson.

In 10th standard, a novel, 'Barrister Parvatheesam' is prescribed as a non-detailed text which is in the form of an autobiography. The sense of patriotism can be seen in the thinking of Parvatheesam and his desire to make the freedom of India as easy task. This can be seen in the reasoning he gave to his father for his journey to England.

Table—5.8 Percentage emphasis to explicit and implicit expression of democratic value

Formula: $\frac{\text{No. of lessons emphasising the expression} \times 100}{\text{Total no. of lessons emphasizing the value}}$

Level/literary form	Explicit/direct expression	Implicit/indirect expression	Eclectic expression
Primary level:			
Prose lessons	36	64	–
Poetry lessons	86	14	–
Secondary level:			
Prose lessons	50	50	–
Poetry lessons	43	57	–
Non-detailed lessons	27	55	18

As seen from Table—5.8, in terms of nature of expression, while there is variation at primary level, the secondary level books appear to be more balanced regarding the explicit and implicit expressions. At primary level, nearly two thirds of the prose lessons use implicit approach, whereas, more than four fifths of the poetry lessons use explicit approach. The secondary level lessons do not show this kind of variation except in non-detailed textbooks which appear to be dependent more upon implicit expression.

Primary Level—Prose Lessons

Five prose lessons have been observed to have used explicit approach in presenting the democratic value at primary level whereas nine lessons are showing implicit nature.

Through the conversation between a boy and his father, the importance of independence day and the love and respect that one should possess towards his country are presented in an explicit manner. The dignity of labour is mentioned very convincingly by the writer in the lesson 'Mana Panini Maname Chesukundam', and the lesson 'Bala Bhatulu' expressed the ideals of scouts. The character of 'Unnava Lakshmi Bai' was exposed by narrating her participation in the freedom movement and the lesson 'Poola Mala' described the beauty of unity. All these five prose lessons are helpful to inculcate the values of democracy with an explicit expression.

It is observed that nine prose lessons are focussing the democratic value with an implicit expression. The lesson 'Aksharala Parichayam' which quotes the advantages of unity needs an explanation to narrate the power of unity. The same aspect is also explained in another lesson' Aikamathyam' through a story of lion and oxen. The symbols of State and Nation also help indirectly to develop the feeling of national integration. The biographies of 'Prakasam' and 'Durga Bai', have an indirect implication with regard to the concept of patriotism. The qualities which are possessed by 'Radha Krishnan' also have an indirect influence with regard to discipline and service to the nation. Need for social justice and equality can be understood by explaining the characteristics of 'Joshua' thoroughly. Through the roles played by small boys in a playlet, the evils of child labour are drawn into light.

Primary Level—Poetry Lessons

It can be found from the Table—5.8 that only poetry lesson reflects the democratic value through implicit expression and all the other six poetry lessons through explicit expression.

The song 'Kalasi Melasi' is based on a story which proves the strength of unity through pictorial illustrations indirectly, and it comes under the category of implicit expression at primary level.

Regarding the explicit expression, the power of unity is rightly mentioned in the context while introducing the alphabets and, a sense of universal brotherhood is directly pointed out by the poet through the poem 'Subhashitalu'. The balled 'Desamunu Preminchumanna' advises every one to be one and love the country in a dedicated manner, and the song 'Sadhistham' is about the pledge taken by the students regarding the aspects of unity, fraternity, harmony, patriotism, discipline and service to the country. The importance of equality is being stressed through all the poems from the lesson

'Samatha', and the second poem of 'Subhashitha Rathnalu' expresses the need for unity and integrity directly or explicitly.

Secondary Level—Prose Lessons

It can be understood from the Table—5.8 that equal emphasis has been given to the prose lessons to focus the Domocratic value with both explicit and implicit expressions.

Duties of a citizen and need for a disciplined life are well expressed through the lesson 'Lekha' and the abolition of male domination is stressed directly in the lesson 'Mundadugu'. The necessity of democratic rule which should be followed for the attainment of world peace is very strictly felt through the lesson 'Prapancha Santhi', and the lesson 'Nayakathvam' explains the real qualifications of a leader. Qualities like self-respect, determination and self-reliance; feelings like social justice, service to the nation and equality can be defined all through the lesson 'Ambedkar'.

In case of implicit expression, five prose lessons at secondary level are identified with the emphasis on democratic value.

The true meaning of patriotism can be known through the character of 'Kesava Rao' during his struggle for independence throughout the lesson 'Sardar Jamalapuram Kesava Rao' in which patriotism is the main theme. In the lesson, 'Lekha' the writer has indirectly suggested some ways and means to face the problems in a democratic society through the role of 'Kaladhar'. The ideals of democracy can be seen indirectly in the lesson 'Suravaram Prathapa Reddy' by the activities of Prathapa Reddy. The concept of socialism and the sense of equality are indirectly highlighted through the character of an old man in a folk tale and the autobiography of 'Sangam Lakshmi Bai' indirectly tells about the feelings of patriotism, and self confidence which she possessed in the lesson 'Na Vishayam'.

Secondary Level—Poetry Lessons

With regard to poetry lessons at secondary level almost equal number of lessons are expressing the value through explicit and implicit manners.

Starting with explicit section, the values of democracy such as frequently, social justice, unity and love for the country are very inspiringly expressed by the poet through the balled 'Samaikya Bharathi'. The concept of equality is very well explained through a song by 'Annamayya' in the lesson 'Parabrahmam'. The message of Gandhiji is straightly conveyed through 'Sandesam', which revealed the ideas of Gandhiji during the time of freedom struggle.

In case of lessons with implicit expression, the feelings of patriotism are conveyed through a beautiful illustration from one poem of 'Chatuvulu', and in the lesson 'Chaldularaginchuta' the impartial attitude of Lord Krishna towards his peer group indirectly strengthens the concept of equality. The agony and sufferings of poor and downtrodden people are sympathetically explained in the lesson 'Kanksha' indirectly through the role of a flower. The ruthless behaviour of the kings is picturised dramatically through the song 'Kanyaka' and the concept of universal love and equality have been stressed indirectly by the role of the girl Kanyaka.

Non-detailed Texts

Table—5.8 reveals that more than half of the total non-detailed lessons are focussing the democratic value through implicit expression and three lessons through explicit and another two through eclectic expressions in this respect.

Regarding the lessons which have explicit expression, the ideas of 'Vemana and Veerabrahmam' about the equality of mankind and greatness of integrity are directly expressed in that lesson. Qualities like service to the nation, education, and love for the country are quoted to be the characteristics of Sweswaraiah' in a direct description by the author. The services of Dr. K.L. Rao towards his constitution and his impartial nature and directly processed by the author.

In case of lessons with implicit expression, the noble ideologies and the except of quest for freedom can be understood through the incidents which which accented in the life of 'Potti Sree Ramulu'. The courage and patriotism of Ramanuja Rao can be understood through his courage of running 'Golkonda' against Nizam Government. Qualities like desire for independence, self dignity and independent nature which are possessed by the queen of 'Jhansi', are reflected in that lesson through various illustrations. The activities related to freedom struggle done by 'Vallabha Bhai Patel', a very determined freedom fighter, are described in the form of various incidents of that lesson. The democratic ideologies and the services of 'Moulana' can be known through his biography in the lesson 'Moulana Abul Kalam Azad'. Lastly, the patriotism behind the thinking of 'Parvatheesam' can be seen at some occasions in his autobiography.

There are two lessons which represent the eclectic expression in focussing the democratic value.

In the lesson 'Tanguturi Prakasam Panthulu' the writer directly mentioned the democratic ideals possessed by Prakasam here and there and there are some references where the writer narrated some illustrations which proved his love and concern for the country. 'Sir C.R. Reddy' directly expressed his views on freedom and independence in the lesson, and there are some instances in this lesson where his love for his motherland, sense of equality, and various other democratic ideals can be understood.

Table—5.9 Percentage emphasis given to the simple and narrative expression of the democratic value

Formula: $\frac{\text{No. of lesson emphasising the expression} \times 100}{\text{Total no. of lessons emphasising the value}}$

Level/literary form	Simple expression	Narrative and situation-oriented expression
Primary level:		
Prose lessons	36	64
Poetry lessons	71	29
Secondary level:		
Prose lessons	60	40
Poetry lessons	43	57
Non-detailed lessons	36	64

The major findings of Table—5.9 in terms of the method of expression are that the secondary level books are giving almost the same emphasis for both the simple and narrative approaches. At primary level, nearly two thirds of the content in prose appears to be using narrative and situation-oriented approach, but, in poetry, nearly three fourths of the content is using simple approach.

At secondary level, there appears to be a balance between these two approaches in prose and poetry lessons and the non-detailed texts have predominantly narrative and situation-oriented approach.

Primary Level—Prose Lessons

At primary level, it can be observed that more number of prose lessons are emphasising the value of democracy through narrative and situation-oriented approach.

With regard to the lessons that are focussing the value through simple approach, only five prose lessons are observed to have come under this category. Enabling to understand the power of unity while introducing an alphabet; developing the spirit of national integration by telling the national and state symbols; inculcating the concept of dignity of labour by illustrating the life of Gandhiji, and mentioning the patriotic nature of 'Durga Bai' are dealt very aptly through simple manner.

Nine prose lessons are observed to focus the characteristics of democracy through narrative and situation-oriented approach.

The importance of independence day and freedom movement are explained in the form of conversation, and the story of a lion and oxen proved the power of unity in their respective lessons. The patriotic nature of 'Prakasam' is well established in his biography, and the aims and ideals of scouts are reminded in the lessons 'Bala Bhatulu'. The ideal nature and the noble characteristics possessed by Dr. S. Radha krishnan and freedom fighter Lakshmi Bai are well focussed. The concept of unity is well treated by the description of a garland in a lesson, and the biography of 'Joshua' revealed his personality through his poetry. Lastly, the evils of child labour are well drawn into light through a small drama.

Primary Level—Poetry Lessons

With regard to poetry lessons, the trend is different as more lessons are focussing the value through simple approach.

The power of unity through a song, and the value of democracy through the poems of 'Subhashithalu' are both explained through simple manner. The duties of students through a balled, the importance of equality through the poems from 'Samata', and the responsibilities of citizens through a song 'Sadhistam' are mentioned in a simple way.

Two poetry lessons at primary level are observed to be emphasizing the aspects of democratic value through narrative manner. The power of unity and integrity is explained by the pictorial illustration in 'Kalasi Melasi' and by the illustration of language through one of the poems from 'Subhashita Rathnalu', in a narrative manner.

Secondary Level—Prose Lessons

Regarding the prose lessons at secondary level, nearly equal weightage has been given for the expression of Democratic value through simple as well as narrative approaches.

The duties of students to become good citizens, the main requirements to achieve world peace; ways and means to go in a right path, the concept of socialism, the qualities of an ideal leader; and the democratic ideals of Ambedkar are mentioned in six prose lessons in a simple manner.

For prose lessons are observed to be emphasising the democratic value through narrative and situation-oriented manner. The message of equality of all human beings is conveyed in the form of a conversation in the lesson 'Mundadugu', and the main theme of patriotism is brought down very well in the form of a biography of 'Kesava Rao'. The freedom struggle done by 'Pratapa Reddy' against Nizam Niwas is described well in his life story and the autobiography of 'Sangam Lakshmi Bai' picturised her noble ideals.

Secondary Level—Poetry Lessons

With regard to poetry lessons at secondary level, almost equal number of lessons can be observed in both the types of expressions to emphasise democratic value.

The patriotic views are expressed simply through the ballad 'Samaikya Bharathi', all the feelings of love for the country have been clearly expressed through the feelings of a flower in a simple manner in another lesson. The message of Gandhiji is also conveyed through the lesson 'Sandesam', in a simple way.

Regarding the narrative expression, one poem from the lesson 'Chatuvulu' gives a clear picture about the sufferings of people of India with a beautiful illustration, and the concept of equality is well depicted by giving so many examples in the song 'Parabrahman', sense of universal brotherhood is well exhibited by the activities of Lord Krishna in the lesson 'Chaldularaginchuta', and through the lesson 'Kanyaka' concepts of justice, truth and fraternity are well explained by the role of 'Kanyaka'.

Non-detailed Texts

It can be found that the number of non detailed lessons that are reflecting the democratic value is more while presenting them in a narrative and situation-oriented manner than the number of lessons which are expressing the value through simple approach.

In case of simple expression, the democratic views, expressed by Vemana and Veerabrahmam, the patriotic ideologies shows by 'Visweswaraih', the political life led by Dr. K.L. Rao, and the flicks of patriotism in the heart of 'Parvatheesam', are presented through the lessons in a simple way.

Regarding the other seven lessons the qualities of democratic value are presented through narrating some incidents from the life stories of those people who have possessed the noble ideologies of democracy.

The biography of 'Prakasam', a great patriot, picturises the democratic ideologies possessed by him in a detailed manner, and the life story of 'Potti Sree Ramulu' analyse the sacrifice done by him in an inspiring manner. The democratic views of 'C.R. Reddy' have been exhibited through some illustrations, and the life story of 'Ramanuja Rao' shows his love for a free democratic country. The prodigious bravery of 'Jhansi Lakshmi Bai', is elucidated through the description of wars which she fought for the freedom of her country. The troubles faced by 'Vallabha Bhai Patel' in the freedom struggle are very well described through various incidents, and the patriotic feelings of 'Moulana Abul Kalam Azad' are very well treated in the lesson through many illustration being given.

Table—5.10 Percentage emphasis given to the chronological periods in presenting the democratic value

Formula: $\frac{\text{No. of lessons emphasising the chronological period} \times 100}{\text{Total no. of lessons emphasising the value}}$

Level/literary form	Contemporary and post independence period	Historical and Pre-independence period
Primary level:		
Prose lessons	64	36
Poetry lessons	86	14
Secondary level:		
Prose lessons	60	40
Poetry lessons	28	72
Non-detailed lessons	9	91

The main findings of Table—5.10 can be noted as that in terms of the preference to the emphasis given to chronological periods, more than two thirds of the emphasis is given at primary level lessons to post-independence period. Nearly four fifths of the content in poetry and two thirds of the prose content at primary level are emphasising post-independence developments to inculcate democratic value.

There is a variation in secondary level content. On the whole, the main focus of the secondary level content is on pre-independence and historical period for inculcating the democratic value. While a little more than half of the content in prose is emphasising on post-independence period, more than four fifths of the non-detailed content and just around three fourths of the poetry content are dependent on pre-independence and historical period to inculcate the democratic value.

Primary Level—Prose Lessons

The prose lessons which are emphasising the democratic value are more dependent on contemporary and post-independence events than the lessons which represent the historical and pre-independence period.

In case of contemporary period, many references that were made in the lessons have revolved around family members and school children. National and state symbols, aims of scouts, and the story of a lion and oxen have been found in some lessons which are contemporary and very well known to all the students.

Regarding the historical period, the people who were mentioned in three lessons have participated in the struggle for Indian independence i.e., Sri Prakasam, Smt. Durga Bai and Smt. Lakshmi Bai. Among the remaining two lessons, one is about Dr. S. Radha Krishnan, the former President of India and the other about Joshua, a very famous poet in Telugu Literature and both of them belong to both pre and post-independence periods.

Primary Level—Prose Lessons

With reference to poetry lessons, from among seven lessons which are emphasising democratic value at primary levei six lessons represent the contemporary and post-independence period.

The lessons, which represent contemporary period consist of poems which are helpful to inculcate the manifestations of democratic value in a universal and general manner whereas there is only one lesson which is in the term of a song and which in fact is a pledge taken by school children towards their motherland.

There is only one lesson in the form of a picture story which represents the historical period and was written in 18th century.

Secondary Level—Prose Lessons

At the secondary level also, the number of prose lessons which represent contemporary and post-independence period to inculcate democratic value is more than the number which represents historical and pre-independence period.

In case of six lessons related to contemporary period, two lessons are in the form of letters written by a father to his son and form a resident of a colony to a news paper editor. There is a biography of Dr. B.R. Ambedkar, an eminent scholar and a social reformer, and another lesson explaining the need for world peace. A lesson in the form of conversation between a grand mother and her grand children, and another lesson in the form of an editorial essay stressing the qualities of leadership also represent this period. All the characters mentioned in the above lessons are contemporary and the incidents are well known to the students.

From among the four lessons related to the historical period, three lessons represent the lives of freedom fighters who belong to pre-independence period and the other lessons is a folk tale. All these four lessons are depending on pre-independence period to inculcate the values of democracy.

Secondary Level—Poetry Lessons

With regard to poetry lessons less number of poetry lessons represent the contemporary period and more the historical age to inculcate democratic value.

Actually, the two poetry lessons Kanksha and Samaikya Bharathi which represent the contemporary period were written in the period of pre-independence. But the aspects that are expressed through those poems are general and universal and may be applicable to any one to inculcate the values of democracy.

In case of poetry lessons which belong to historical age three lessons namely Chatuvulu, Kanyaka and Sandesam represent the events which happened in the period of pre-independence. 'Parabrahman' is a song written by Annamayya who belongs to 14th century and 'Chaldularaginchuta' is a mythological lesson which has a story of Lord Krishna.

Non-detailed Texts

As seen from Table—5.10 only one lesson from the non-detailed texts, prescribed at the secondary level represents the contemporary period which deals with the biography of Ramanuja Rao, a person well known for his love for literature and who belong to 20th century post-independence period.

From among the ten lessons at the historical age, nine lessons have shown some of the great personalities of India who possessed great ideologies, patriotism and dedication and all these persons represent the period of pre-independence . Only one lesson namely, 'Vemana and Veerabrahman' represents the period of 16th century which comes under historical period.

Secular Values

The frequency of occurrances of the manifestations of the secular value, the mode of various expressions of that particular value and the emphasis given to the chronological contexts to present the value are tabulated and interpreted through the following 5.11, 5.12, 5.13 and 5.14 tables.

Table—5.11 **Manifestation of secular value frequency of occurrence**

Manifestation	Primary level		Secondary level		
	Prose	Poetry	Prose	Poetry	Non-detailed
1. Respect for all religions	2	2	2	3	8
2. Tolerance of others' beliefs	1	1	2	3	7
3. Promotion of rational outlook	1	1	2	1	5
4. Freedom from fanaticism	1	–	3	5	2
5. Duty to society in a spirit of harmony	2	–	2	3	6

It is evident from Table—5.11 that there is less emphasis on secular value at both the levels.

Highest emphasis is given to the characteristic of respect for all religions followed by tolerant behaviour of other's views, where as less emphasis can be seen as given to the characteristic of promotion of rational outlook.

There have been no references made in the poetry lessons at primary level regarding the characteristics of freedom from fanaticism and duty towards society with harmony.

To illustrate and substantiate the above findings, the following instances from the textbooks are detailed here under.

Primary Level

Regarding secular values at this level, more emphasis is given to show the respect towards all religious. A poem from the ballad 'Desamunu Preminchumanna' throws light on the fruits of living together forgetting all the communal disparities and variations in caste and religion. This poem advises all the people to live together like a close knit family with the feeling of respect towards all religions.

The lesson 'Muddabanthi Poolu' comprises the value of secularism in almost in the whole of the lesson which is in the form of a conversation between teachers and students who do not belong to a single religion. The role of 'Sankaram' teacher defines religion as a path which guides people towards what is good and which develops a good character in a person and he thus develops the attitude of love and respect towards all religions.

The other lesson 'Bala Seva Sangham' is in fact two letters, one written by a grand father to his grandson and the other the reply by the grandson who is a student. In his reply, the boy mentioned about the activities of their association that they treat children belonging to various religions with equal love and care while they were hospitalised. True secular value of showing respect for others' religions can be found here.

Need for possessing tolerant attitude towards others' religions, views and opinions are emphasised through some of the references. A poem from the ballad at 3rd standard directly the need for tolerant attitude towards all religions by advising all the people to live together.

In the lesson 'Muddabanthi Poolu' even the students show true secularism in their conversation. The message of the lesson is to love all people equally without any religious disparities and to have tolerant attitude towards others' customs and cultures.

Promotion of rational outlook is emphasised through some references at this level. The lesson 'Joshua' reveals the poet Joshua's personality as a man who fought against superstitious beliefs of the people. He shunned the people who depend on other persons or even God to do their chores and advised them to believe in themselves. The poetry lessons 'Samatha' emphasises the idea of secularism in a very efficient manner. The poet tells that though there are many religious disparities, we all belong to one race of the human race. Though there are many castes, the people are one the Indians. Though there are many groups, the ultimate feeling is one, the humanity. Through this explanation the poet tries to develop rational outlook among the traders.

Developing the attitude of duty mindedness towards society with harmony is focussed through some references at primary level. In the lesson 'Unnava Lakshmi Bai' Smt. Lakshmi Bai is known as a woman trying to protect secular values which are diminishing in the present society. She strived to spread the concept of unity among all the people around her. The poet 'Joshua' fought his battle with his pen. He wrote poetry not about nature and its beauty but about society and its evils. He advised people to believe in themselves and work hard for the benefit of themselves and the society instead of waiting for the unseen God to do something.

Need for having freedom from fanaticism is emphasised through the lesson 'Unnava Lakshmi Bai' at 4th standard. Smt. Lakshmi Bai fought against child marriages and tried real hard to derive away the devil called untouchability.

Secondary Level

Developing the attitude of having freedom from fanaticism is stressed through more references at secondary level. In the lesson 'Lekha' a father explained to his son about the bad endings caused by the superstitious beliefs through a letter. The lesson 'Mundadugu' is a conversation between a girl Hima, her brother Pavan and their grandmother. The superstitious beliefs of the people in olden days such as child marriages, dowry system, Sati Sahagamana, etc., have been criticised through their conversation and emphasised the need for the freedom from fanaticism. A poem from the balled 'Samaikya Bharathi' specified that being particular about religion is nothing but stupidity and further stated that religious customs and restrictions will drive away humanity and thus stressed the aspect of having freedom from fanaticism. The writer of the lesson 'Kashta Jeevi' writes that the whole country is indebted to the people of backward the scheduled class. He criticises the Zamandari system and the ban on these people to enter the temples and he greatly degrades the concept of untouchability.

The poetry lesson 'Kanksha' is about the desire of a flower. The flower opens its heart and exposes its feelings. It wishes that people should not place it at the feet of the statues of Gods. It says that what lives in temples is nothing but stone statues which are just created by the rich people to fulfil their pride.

Another poetry lesson 'Ambedkar' narrates that Dr. Ambedkar wrote in our constitution to abolish the caste system. The evils of the absurd systems of the society that have prevailed in those days and the benefits of a secular system can be nearly inferred from this lesson. A prose lesson 'Ambedkar Vyakthithvam' at 10th standard also picturises the pain and agony of Dr. Ambedkar in his childhood days as he was looked down by all the people regarding his birth in a low caste family. He was highly insulted and outcast by the society which shows the level of stupidity in the people of those days and emphasizes the need for having freedom from such fanaticism.

In a poem from the poetry lesson 'Subhashithalu' the poet writes that all the so called Astrology, Numerology, Horoscope, etc., are all man made things which he made to fill his stomach. The poet feels that the future of tomorrow depends on the deeds of today and thus advised people to develop self-confidence and get free from such fanaticisms.

Need for possessing love and respect towards all religions is emphasized through some references of secondary level. The lesson 'Lekha' which is in the form of two letters written by a father to his son and the son's reply shows the father's view regarding the evils of communal clashes and religious variations. The father advises his son to feel concern for those suffering from these clashes and help them with his friends and thus stresses the concept of love and respect to be shown towards other religions which may help to stop those communal clashes.

The impartial nature of 'Lakshmana Rao' towards the people who belonged to various religious, races and countries can be observed while he wrote about the histories of great people. The promotion of tolerant attitude and respect for all religious is hereby seen through the lesson 'Komarraju Lakshmana Rao'.

Two poems from 'Subhashithalu' lay a good measure of stress on the absurd religious and lack of secularism. The poet further questions that while food is the most essential requirement of every person and the want of food or hunger is same to all, why should people keep the barriers of religion between them?

Developing the attitude of tolerance towards others' religions, their views and opinions is focussed through some references at this level. In the lesson 'Lekha' the evils of communal clashes and religious variations are mentioned by the role of a father who advised his son to feel concern for those who are suffering from the communal clashes and also told him that such incidents should not be encouraged. 'Kashta Jeevi' is another lesson written by poet 'Joshua'. He writes about the social and communal inequalities and mentioned that the society should not shun the downtrodden and backward class people regarding their castes and he thus emphasised the need for showing tolerant attitude towards people of other castes.

The lesson 'Ambedkar' also shows the life of the backward class people during Ambedkar's childhood days. The poet illicited very clearly all the problems they faced in those days due to their low caste. This shows the peak level of the stupid superstitions of those people in a very pathetic way and stressed the need for having tolerance towards other people and their castes.

Need for developing the attitude of duty mindedness towards society with harmony is emphasised through some references at the secondary level. The ideologies of a father that are expressed through his letter to his son in the lesson 'Lekha' explained clearly about the concern he had for those who are suffering from communal clashes. He advised his son to go to the villages along with his classmates to enlighten the illiterates about the superstitious beliefs and bad practices that they were under.

In the lesson 'Mundadugu' the services rendered by the social reformers are mentioned through the role of a girl. This lesson helps to promote service mindedness towards the society.

The poet Joshua expressed his views in the lesson 'Kashta Jeevi' about the social and communal inequalities and he tells that instead of spending huge amounts of money for the festivals and marriages of Gods lavishly it will be very kind to give the poor people some of that money and thus evoked the sense of service towards the society.

The life story of Ambedkar reveals the ignorance and folly of the people in those days. After Dr. Ambedkar became famous, he tried so hard to remove those barriers between the people and he craved to see his people mingle freely with all other people in the society.

Promotion of rational outlook is emphasised through a few references at secondary level. The lesson 'Kashta Jeevi' explains the rational outlook of the secret 'Joshua' when he asks the people to abolish idol worship and advises them to donate a little of their earnings to the poor people. In another lesson. 'Mundadugu' the role of the girl Hima tells her brother and grandmother about the services done by eminent social reformers of India who fought against child marriages, sati Sahagamana and who promoted widow marriages and education for girls. She advises that all people should stop believing in such dirty superstitions and promote rational outlook.

The lesson 'Ambedkar Vyakthithvam' shows that the people were so hardly treated in the days of Dr. Ambedkar. The feeling of backwardness and outcasting was rooted so deep in their minds that they psychologically considered themselves worth nothing and they never believed in themselves. At that time Dr. Ambedkar came to their rescue and awakened their dead spirits and thus tried to promote rational outlook among them.

Non-detailed Texts

In case of non-detailed texts, more emphasis is laid on the manifestation of respect for all religions and the characteristic of freedom from fanaticism.

It is very interesting to note that all the five manifestations of secular value have all occurred in the lesson 'Vemana and Veerabrahmam' at 6th standard. Both the social reformers openly criticised the stupid superstitions of the people and had many disciples who belonged to all religions. They pleaded the people to have rational outlook and preached the fruits of unity and integrity among people irrespective of their castes and religions.

In the lesson 'Mokshagundam Visvesvaraiah' his services to the society, abolition of caste system, development of rational outlook, and denouncement of child marriages and dowry system reflect the three manifestations very aptly. 'Mother Teresa' threw light on the point that service is better than prayer and her secularism can be understood from the fact that despite being a Christian, she came to live in India among Hindus and served them all alike.

'Potti Sree Ramulu' tried for the uplifting of scheduled castes and tribes, fought for the abolition of the untouchability, and taught that the castes and religions should be banned as they create distances within the single human race.

The same three manifestations of Secular value are also seen in the lesson 'Sir C.R. Reddy' who promoted rational outlook, showed tolerant attitude towards others views, served the society, and taught the people to treat all people equally.

The life of the famous engineer 'K.L. Rao' shows that untouchability is a very big evil and it should not be encouraged. He also seen to be allowing his children to get married irrespective of their castes, religion and thus proved his secular ideologies.

The manifestations of respect for all religions and duty towards society are focussed in the lesson 'Jhansi Lakshmi Bai' by telling that all the kings of India both Hindus and Muslims came together and swore to fight together against British rulers.

Need to develop broadmindedness and respect for all religions can be seen in the lesson 'Sardar Vallabha Bhai Patel' while narrating the incident which leads to the division of India due to the clashes between people belonging to two different religions. Characteristics like respect for all religions and broadmindedness are focussed in the three non detailed lessons of the 9th standard. All the three great personalities of these lessons Sri Krishna Deva Rayalu, King of Vijayanagar Empire, Sathyalingam Nayakar, an eminent philanthropist, and Doctor Subba Rao have shown their imperial nature while dealing with people from different religious backdrops.

Table—5.12 Percentage of emphasis given to explicit and implicit expression of secular value

Formula: $\frac{\text{No. of lessons emphasising the expression} \times 100}{\text{Total No. lessons emphasising the value}}$

Level/literary form	Explicit expression	Implicit expression
Primary level:		
Prose lessons	50	50
Poetry lessons	100	–
Secondary level:		
Prose lessons	75	25
Poetry lessons	40	60
Non-detailed lessons	36	64

Table—5.12 shows that equal emphasis was given to both explicit and implicit expressions of secular value at primary level prose lessons where as in the poetry lessons the emphasis was given only to explicit expression. In case of the lessons at secondary level, three fourth of the total emphasis was given to explicit expression at prose section and the situation is quite opposite in poetry section which shows that two thirds of the total emphasis is for implicit and one thirds for explicit expression.

The non-detailed texts also have shown the similar condition with two thirds of the emphasis for implicit and one thirds for explicit expression of secular value.

Primary Level

At the primary level regarding the prose lessons with explicit expression, the manifestations of secularism like respect for all religions, and tolerant attitude towards others' opinions expressed directly by the role of a master through the lesson 'Muddabanthi Poolu'. The same ideas are directly expressed through a student in the form of a letter in another lesson 'Bala Seva Sangham'.

In case of poetry lessons at primary level, more emphasis was given to the concept of unity among mankind forgetting all the communal disparities and variations in caste and religion which are expressed through the feelings of the poets through the ballad 'Desamunu Preminchumanna' and the lesson 'Samatha'.

Only prose lessons have shown emphasis on implicit expression at primary level.

While explaining the services rendered by 'Lakshmi Bai' towards society, and the ideologies of 'Joshua' regarding superstitious beliefs, the manifestations of secularism are such that they should be drawn into light while teaching the lessons 'Unnava Lakshmi Bai' and 'Joshua'.

Secondary Level

At the secondary level regarding the explicit expression at prose lessons, manifestations of secularism, like respect for all religions and tolerance of others' views are directly emphasised through a role of a father in the lesson 'Lekha'. In the lesson

'Mundadugu' characteristics like promotion of rational outlook, freedom from fanaticism and duty towards society are well established through a conversation between a girl, a boy and their grandmother. While describing the personality of 'Ambedkar' the writer directly expressed the secular attitude of Ambedkar in the lesson 'Ambedkar Vyakthithvam'.

Only one prose lesson called 'Komarraju Lakshmana Rao' has implicit expression of secular value at secondary level in which students should be taught about the broadmindedness of Lakshmana Rao by explaining the imperial nature shown by him while writing books.

In case of poetry lessons at secondary level, two lessons have emphasised the value through explicit expression. The concept of freedom from fanaticism and promotion of rational outlook are stressed in the ballad 'Samaikya Bharathi' and along with these ideas, respect for all religions was also expressed directly in the poem taken from 'Subhashitha Ratnalu'.

Three poetry lessons have shown the implicit expression of secular value at secondary level. The need for secularism is felt through the description of the fate and ill treatment faced by a backward, downtrodden person in the Indian society through the poems of 'Kashta Jeevi'.

While explaining the feelings of a flower in the poems of 'Kanksha' the dignity of service which rendered for the sake of society can be noted.

Through the description of the life story of Ambedkar the poet indirectly cautioned the need and necessity of true secularism in the Indian society through the balled 'Ambedkar'.

Non-detailed Texts

Regarding the lessons of non-detailed texts, four lessons represented the explicit section and the rest seven have implicit expression of secular value at secondary level.

The preachings of 'Vemana and Veerabrahmam' which possessed the characteristics of true secularism have direct and explicit expression.

The reformities taken by 'Visweswaraiah' are also expressed directly regarding the abolition of caste system and child marriages. The author expressed his views about Mother Teresa for her services and tolerant attitude in an explicit manner.

In case of 'Sree Krishna Deva Rayalu' also, the secular ideologies and attempts of that famous king are directly described by the author.

More emphasis was given to the implicit expression of secular value at secondary value non-detailed texts because of the reason that all reasons are nothing but the biographies of eminent people. While regarding their life stories students need the co-operation in the form of explanation to understand the hidden values that are reflected through so many incidents and illustrations quoted by the authors.

The secular values like promotion of rational outlook, broadmindedness, and duty towards society with harmony could be explained through the lessons 'Potti Sree Ramulu' and 'Sir C.R. Reddy'. Feelings of respect for all religions and tolerance could be explained while teaching the lesson 'Dr. K.L. Rao'. The attitude of Hindu and Muslims kings in the lesson 'Jhansi Lakshmi Bai' indirectly provoked the sense of respect for all religions and duty towards society with harmony. The incident of the division of country due to the lack of communal harmony indirectly warned the necessity of secularism through the lesson 'Sardar Vallabha Bhai Patel'.

The two non detailed lessons from 9th standard 'Sathya Lingam Nayakar' and 'Dr. Y. Subbarao', indirectly expressed the manifestation of respect for all religions by narrating some incidents in the biographies of these two great persons.

As seen from the Table—5.13 three fourth of the prose lessons have chosen a simple way to express the secular value where as only one fourth of the prose lessons expressed the value in a narrative way at both primary and secondary level.

Table—5.13 Percentage emphasis given to simple and narrative expression of secular value

Formula: $\frac{\text{No. of lessons with simple or narrative expression} \times 100}{\text{Total No. of lessons emphasising the value}}$

Level/literary form	Simple expression	Narrative/situation oriented expression
Primary level:		
Prose lessons	75	25
Poetry lessons	100	–
Secondary level:		
Prose lessons	75	25
Poetry lessons	80	20
Non-detailed lessons	45	55

There is no representation for the narrative expression of poetry lessons at primary level and only one poetry lesson has expressed the value in the narrative manner at secondary level.

In case of non-detailed texts, almost equal emphasis was given to the simple and narrative expressions of the secular value at secondary level.

Primary Level

At the primary level the secular ideologies of 'Unnava Lakshmi Bai' and 'Joshua', and the services rendered by the 'Bala Seva Sangham' are expressed in a simple way. Whereas, in the lesson 'Muddabanthi Poolu' concepts like respect to be shown towards other religions, definition of a real religion, equal treatment to be given to all religions are explained in a narrative way by the conversation of a school teacher with his students. In the poetry section, the two poets and the ballads, 'Desamunu Preminchumanna' and 'Samatha' advised people to show tolerant attitude towards other religions and to develop rational outlook in a simple way.

Secondary Level

At the secondary level, the views of a father regarding the evils of communal clashes and religious variations are expressed in the lesson 'Lekha' in a simple say. The concepts of freedom from fanaticism and promotion of rational outlook are simply explained in the lesson 'Mundadugu' through a conversation among the members of a family. The same ideas are also emphasised in the lesson 'Ambedkar Vyakthithvam' in a simple way. While writing about the autobiography of 'Komarraju Lakshmana Rao' the author narrated the impartial treatment of Sri Laksmana Rao towards the people of other religions through some incidents in the lesson.

Four poetry lessons are found to have expressed the secular value in a simple way and only one lesson by a narrative manner. The need for the freedom from fanaticism is emphasised simply through the balled 'Samaikya Bharthi' and the same idea along with developing respect towards other religions is expressed through the role of a flower in the lesson 'Kanksha' in a simple fashion. All the manifestations of secularism are expressed simply through the balled, 'Ambedkar' and need for developing tolerant attitude and respect towards other religious are expressed by the poems of 'Subhashithalu' in a simple format.

'Kastha Jeevi' is the only poetry lesson at secondary level which emphasised the manifestations of secularism in a narrative manner by narrating the life of a person who is backward and downtrodden.

In case of non-detailed lessons, equal emphasis was given to the lessons which have expressed the value of secularism both in simple and narrative manners.

The ideologies of secularism possessed by 'Vemana and Veerabrahmam', 'Mokshagundam Visweswaraiah' and 'Mother Teresa' are expressed in a simple way in 6th standard. Sense of duty mindedness and respect for all religions which are shown by 'Jhansi Lakshmi Bai' and 'Dr. Subbarao' are also expressed in a simple manner in 8th and 9th standards. Whereas, the biographies of 'Potti Sree Ramulu', 'Sir C.R. Reddy', 'K.L. Rao', 'Vallabha Bhai Patel', Andhra Bhojudu' and 'Satyalingam Nayakar' who followed the principles of secularism all through their lives are explained in the lessons in a narrative manner.

Table—5.14 Percentage emphasis given to the chronological periods in presenting the secular value

Formula: $\frac{\text{No. of lessons emphasising the period x 100}}{\text{Total No. of lessons emphasising the value}}$

Level/literary form	Contemporary and post independence period	Historical and pre-independence period
Primary level:		
Prose lessons	50	50
Poetry lessons	50	50
Secondary level:		
Prose lessons	50	50
Poetry lessons	20	80
Non-detailed lessons	9	91

It is interesting to note that the findings of Table—5.14 have shown that equal emphasis was given to the chronological periods in presenting the values of secularism at both primary and secondary levels. But it is little sad to see that very less emphasis was given to the non-detailed lessons which have expressed the values of secularism of the contemporary and post-independence period. Obviously only one lesson represented this period and the others belong to the historical period.

Regarding the lessons related to contemporary period, the roles played by a teacher and students, the characters of a grand mother and grand children in a playlet; and the roles of a grand father, a father, a grand son and a son in the two lessons which are in the form of letters are very similar to the students in their day-to-day normal life. The ballads, 'Desamunu Preminchumanna' and 'Samaikya Bharathi' also come under this category which emphasise the need for religious tolerance though they were written in the pre-independence period.

The lessons which come under the category of historical and pre-independence period are nothing but the biographies of freedom fighters like Lakshmi Bai, Joshua, Ambedkar and

Lakshmana Rao who practised the principles of secularism and actually all of them belong to pre-independence period.

'Subhashithalu' is the only lesson which was written in 17th century and the poems collected from sonnets preach the need for freedom from fanaticism.

Among the non-detailed texts only one lesson represents the contemporary period which is 'Mother Teresa'. Among the lessons which come under the category of historical period 'Vemana and Veerabrahamam', 'Andhra Bhojudu' are the two lessons which represent the period of 6th century. The rest of the lessons which have the main focus on the biographies of great and famous people belong to pre-independence period.

Conclusions

The aim of education should be the growth of the individual through truthful life without neglecting the welfare and progress of the society and the nation's cherished ideals of freedom, equality and social justice. To this end, education should strengthen the values of democracy, secularism, and socialism apart from moral behaviour.

At the very outset, it can be concluded from the primary value data classifications, that the inculcation of moral, democratic, and secular value manifestations in the Telugu textbook material is very dismal. Only moral value seems to have been given a semblance of some consideration.

Regarding the illustrations, most of the instances of value manifestations, examples of which are reported in the analysis, are based on stories, social and historical, and to some extent conversations between certain characters.

It can be seen from the study that moral values are given greater emphasis than the other two values, and at times, nearly equal importance to the combined effect of democratic and secular values at all standards of instruction. It is, therefore, gratifying to note that Telugu content writers are very conscious of imparting moral values among children which by implication project religious and ethical values as well. A steady and a sustained effort has been made all along the standards from standard 1 to 10 to bring in moral concepts as and when it is possible in the Telugu textbook content.

The second important value that attached the attention of the authors is democratic value which is more or less evenly distributed at all levels barring one single exception at standard 6. Democracy is a more complex concept than the moral concept. Children are not exposed to democratic functioning at any stage of their development at home and in the school. The rules and regulations, the traditional restrictions and social customs all point out to a tame docility rather than enable the child to develop individuality with all its ramifications of freedom and liberty. This, being the philosophical belief of the adults who impress the children, school textbooks do not differ from this stance at all. Hence are the lower levels of democratic value manifestations in the Telugu textbook. However, as the nation is preparing into the 21st century with democratic administration of the state functioning effectively in the life of a citizen, the textbook could not but bring in some references that highlight the value of democracy.

Secularism again is most difficult of the three to comprehend even for a grown up citizen let alone the children of schools. There has been a great deal of debate on the nature and scope of secularism even today in the political and intellectual circles. Though Kothari (1964) in the famous Education Commission has clarified that secularism is not an irreligious state of affairs, but offering equal importance and opportunity of all religious beliefs to flourish conditional protection, still people doubt whether there is anything possible. Though feeble, the attempts of the authors of the Telegu textbooks are laudable in the wake of this uncertainty. A broad approach to the beliefs of the individuals, or groups, their culture, and life styles is emphasized through definite, though sparing instances.

It can also be concluded that the writers of the textbooks have exercised greater freedom to bring in the moral values in the non-detailed textbook content than in prose and poetry forms which are, in a way, selections from literature. Almost all the sixteen identified moral value manifestations have been reflected to some extent or other in the non-detailed lessons. As expected on the basis of the social fabric of the community, servicemindedness, good character, and love and concern for others have been amply considered, strangely, to the neglect of non-violence and truthfulness.

A probe into the nature of the content classified into explicit or direct and implicit or indirect has not revealed any particular noticeable tendency on the part of the writers except in the poetry lessons at the primary level, where, attempts are seen to present moral values explicitly as the children at that stage can better understand direct manifestations rather than extract values from implied contexts.

A point of interest of the present study is to find out whether the writers are making it simple for the students to grasp the value or whether they are presenting the value through descriptions and contexts in an extended situation. On the basis of data so classified it can be concluded that narrative and situation oriented expressions of the values are predominantly used in the context except, again, in the case of primary poetry lessons where simplicity, which enables the children at that level to understand the value easily, dominated the writers' intentions.

As an ancillary consideration, the moral values identified from the content are categorised into material related to contemporary life of the children or taken from historical documentation. It can be concluded here with a great deal of satisfaction that a large number of values referred to or related to contemporary period enabling the child to apply and assimilate the values in terms of known and immediate experiences. Only in the case of non-detailed lessons, where stories dominate the content historical perspectives are overwhelmingly represented.

Democratic value is also subjected to similar treatment analysis. It can be seen that the democratic value has been occurring almost with equal emphasis at the two levels of the study and in the three forms of presentation. Inculcation of the spirit of patriotism and freedom have dominated the democratic value content material. Schools which lay undue emphasis on discipline do not find their support from the Telegu textbooks where disciplinary value is the lowest.

In the democratic value also, the results revealed almost the same state in the explicit-implicit classification with poetry at the primary level projecting values explicitly and directly thereby enhancing children's understanding at the level.

The same trend which was seen in the moral value presentation is also reflected in the democratic value as far as the simple and narrative expressions are concerned. The primary level poetry lessons contain simple expressions of democratic values and the rest presented through descriptions, styles and grammar of their own. The primary students' levels of understanding have been borne in mind by the writers.

The content material with the democratic value goes along with the same lines as moral value. The predominant instances of value manifestations are from contemporary experiences enabling the child to be at home with the value conceptions, except in the non-detailed textbook where the content of the stories invariably related to historical and pre-independence situations.

Secular value considerations also reflect noticeable trends in favour of greater emphasis to religious harmony and tolerance to different beliefs. These are embedded in the Indian constitution and are required very much in the present day national situation where communalism and religionalism are raising their ugly heads. There should have been greater emphasis on the curtailment of fanaticism which is given lowest emphasis.

In slight variation to the observations on the moral and democratic values more importance was given to explicit presentation at the secondary level also along with the primary poetry which has commended the total attention of the writers.

Again, a slight deviation from the previous situations can be seen in the secular value presentations which are expressed abundantly through simple expressions for the reason that a secular value which is not so familiar with the child's experience so far has to be expressed in simple and understandable terms. It can be concluded that the writers have been deliberately making efforts to instill secular foundations in the growing children which is a healthy and positive sign.

Presentation of secular values through contemporary and historical material has also received some differential treatment. Almost equal importance is given to contemporary and historical events of the secular value manifestations in both the levels, except, of course, in the non-detailed material which again have drown its sources from historical documentation.

Generalisations

On the basis of the various conclusions drawn from the findings it can be generalised that the content material in the Telugu textbooks of the primary and secondary schools do not reflect the values, moral value, democratic and secular, to the extent they are required to keep in view the aims and objectives of education with special reference to the teaching of mother tongue at the school level. Further, it is gratifying to generalise that some consideration has been given to the inculcation of moral value to the neglect of democratic and secular values.

It can also be generalised with a self-satisfaction that most of value manifestations presented are related to the immediate and contemporary experiences of the children.

6

Executive Summary

Introduction

Almost every education commission released before and after the independence of India have stressed the need for teaching the values such as social, moral, and spiritual. The University Education Commission (1948) stressed the inclusion of spiritual training in education.

The Mudaliyar Education Commission (1953) confirmed the place of values in the development of character. Kothari Education Commission (1964-66) emphasised the selection of values which determines the future of the society.

The greatest challenge before Indian education is to inculcate in the people a scientific temper, an unwavering commitment to the values of national integration, equality, human dignity and universal brotherhood ignoring all barriers of caste, creed, gender, religion, language and region.

Values play a very dominant part motivating and sustaining the active and concrete contribution of a person to himself and to others. Kluckhohn (1957) defined value as a conception, explicit or implicit distinctive of an individual or characteristic of a group of the desirable, which influences the selection from available modes and ends of action.

Rokeach (1973) explained value as an enduring belief, a specific mode of conduct or end sate existence along a continuum of relative importance.

Pepper (1958) going along the same lines interprets values as a selection process.

Values are yardstick of beliefs that influence our behaviourism and help in the making of choices. A value can itself be defined as a belief, which guides human behaviour and helps in making decisions about choices.

Value Education

Education must initiate a life long process of developmental exploration within its two dimensions, one of the self and the second of the community and the wider society. This emphasises the need for value education.

The youth of our country are confronted with disintegrating values. One of the effective tools to revitalise our youth and bring meaning and purpose in life is value education. Value education, which needs to be looked upon as an essential aspect for the overall qualitative improvement of education, is being neglected to a great extent.

In the process of learning different curricular subjects, one comes to imbibe certain values, habits of thought, qualities of mind that are concommitment to the pursuit of that particular knowledge field. In other words, value education spans the entire learning, cultivation of imagination, strengthening of will, and training of character. When we so relate value education to education, we can identify the approach as one of integrating values into the very fabric of education.

Classification of Values

Educationists as well as philosophers defined values in different ways and also classified differently using various criteria. Broadly, a comprehensive and elegant classification is propounded by the National Educational Policy (1986) of the Government of India which classified all these values into three main categories namely, personal values, social values and national values which are mutually exclusive and all inclusive. The commission highlights these three as essential and fundamental values for the purposes of education, specially at the school level.

Personal values may be defined as the values which guide an individual towards what is enriching and good for him. These values would be what an individual accepts as ideals, which govern his style of living. These are practised by the individual alone irrespective of his or her social relationships. Personal values can be classified as moral values, spiritual values, ethical values, aesthetic values, knowledge values and so on. Of these, moral value is predominantly influential and conditions the other values such as spiritual, ethical etc. As stressed by Sri Prakasa Committee (1959), every effort must therefore be made to teach students true moral values from the earliest stages of their educational life. But these values cannot be strictly taught in a formal manner in the classrooms but they are learnt by students through the curriculum, textbooks, example, demonstrations and environmental interactions. Moral values can also be, incidentally and deliberately taught through literature and students may be allowed to discuss certain moral characters in the literature to which they are exposed.

Social values can be defined as the ideals which the society expects its members to observe in their day today life. The youth of today and tomorrow should be imbued with a strong commitment to social values. From among cultural, literary, scientific and secular values which come under social values, secular values would need much more focus and ample attention for the present generation. The five most essential educational objectives of secularism are—respect for all religious, tolerance of other's opinions and views, freedom from fanaticism and narrowness of outlook, promotion of a rational and objective frame of mind; the duty to self and society in a spirit of harmony and well-being.

The values which involve the survival of the nation are national values and the practice of such values is very essential for the growth of any nation. Since India has decided to make itself a democratic republic, the citizens have to be trained to uphold and practice the values of democratic social order. This feeling can be developed in students through education which has democratic values like equality, participation, harmony and corporate building up of the nation. Democratic education, however, is a life long process operating from the cradle to the grave besides being life wide as well, operating in home, street, school and almost every social organisation.

Sources of Value Education

Values are obtained or inculcated through certain informal, non-formal and formal sources. The values identified for a systematic study in this investigation namely moral, secular and democratic values, are initiated and promoted through some agencies like the family, the society and in the final analysis the school through the instrumentalities of teacher and the curriculum.

Language enables a person to understand the feelings of others and express his inner views. Many of the educational values like literary, moral, political, social, scientific, democratic, secular, religious, cultural, aesthetic, humorous, historical and others can be inculcated thoroughly through the teaching of language.

One of the most frequent used methods of selecting educational material is that of adopting a textbook and teaching the materials contained in it. Textbook are books which are designed to present the basic principles or aspects of a given subject of use as a basis of instruction. But, contents have to be updated and made relevant to the needs of society and the material taught must be challenging enough to involve and develop the young minds.

Among languages, the highest importance is to be given to the mother tongue. Education through mother tongue needs to be ensured because it is an important medium for inculcating, fostering and propagating the moral values and national and cultural heritage. Literature is a vehicle for training the character and inculcating the right sense of values through the study of literary masterpieces and communication with the spirit of great writers.

Need for the Study

Language and literature hold a significant place in the whole system of values. Language textbooks in mother tongue which promote desirable values for the present society are considered extremely necessary for the school education system.

The present investigation is mainly aimed at studying the realisation of moral, secular and democratic values in the present school level textbooks in mother tongue from standard one to ten of Andhra Pradesh.

In order to help men and women develop right kin of value systems, the implications of the textual content matter supplied to the future generation is a matter of grave concern. In the Indian setting, most of the children stop their education at the end of the secondary stage. Students at this level are at the formative stage. Unless they are grounded in proper values, their future will be bleak and disturbed. It is expected that when the students at the end of their ten-year student career enter the wider arena of life, they must be fully equipped with the right values of life.

Review of related literature, points out that textbooks are analysed in the past in many ways for many purposes. The emphasis of such efforts was mainly on issues such as the quality of the textbooks, the enrichment of vocabulary, the portrayal of women in the content and an appreciation of prose and poetry in school children. But, studies which focussed on the school textbooks as sources of values important were not attempted.

The research questions for this piece of study are: Are the textbooks in mother tongue suitable for the realisation of moral, secular and democratic values? Is the content reflecting the manifestations of the values? And, does the content reflect planned approach for presenting the value?

The title of this study is "An Evaluation of the Realisation of Moral, Democratic and Secular Values in the Textbook Content in Telegu Language at Primary and Secondary Schools Levels in Andhra Pradesh".

Objectives of the Study

The study is based upon the following major objectives:

1. To examine the extent to which moral, secular and democratic values are being given importance in the current school level textbooks of mother tongue.
2. To study the extent to which these values are being realised in prose lessons.
3. To study the extent to which the poetry lessons are realising these values.
4. To study the extent to which these values are being realised in non-detailed textbooks lessons.

Scope and Limitations of the Study

1. The present study is limited to the textbooks of mother tongue at primary and secondary levels of Andhra Pradesh which are at present prescribed and used.
2. The values which are taken into account for the present study are moral, secular and democratic which are considered, as discussed earlier, as most significant and comprehensive.

Review of Related Literature

A review of related literature provides a deeper understanding of the nature, scope and significance of the study. The investigator reviewed related literature and studies done in both abroad and India to give an insightful understanding of the problem and the highlights are reported here.

Pandya (1959) measured modern values from different stand points, whereas Ahmad (1973) studied the relationship between values and modernity. Reddy (1976), Diwedi (1983) and Tarlok Singh (1983) have studied the role of education in developing the values.

There has been some research work done regarding the values of students, exclusively. Kalia (1970) made a research on ego ideals and values of students and Gaur (1975) studied values and perceptions of high school students. Gosh's (1977) study was based on distribution of social values among youth and Patel (1981) and Zamen (1982) studied the prevalent value system of students.

There are few researchers in the area of religion, religious values, and religious education. Tandon (1967) studied the attitudes of students towards religion and Rizvi (1986) made a research on the study of attitudes towards religious education.

There are a few studies in the area of moral instruction. Seetha Ramu (1974) conducted an experiment on the study of moral instruction and Gopalaih (1981) made a study on moral judgement in children.

There are some studies regarding the values related to democratic values. Singh, R.P. (1960) made a research on democracy and higher secondary education in Uttar Pradesh, whereas Singh, A.K. (1980) has done a research on political attitudes of college students.

In the Nagarjuna University, three researches were done on the educational values in Telegu literature. Prabhavathi (1994) studied educational values in children's literature. Satyavathi's (1995) research was on the 'Study of Educational Values in Telugu Novels' and Sai Leela (1996) made a research on 'The Realisation of Educational Values in Ancient Telugu Sathakas'.

There are so many studies regarding the basic vocabulary of school children. Chandra Sekharaiah (1964) studied the basic vocabulary of elementary school children and Kathardekar's (1982) research was on the basic vocabulary of 7th standard students.

Study of critical evaluation of textbooks was done by Pinge (1972) and Chaudhari (1977). Evaluation of Telugu language textbooks was done by Linga Reddy (1987) at intermediate level and Prasad (1991) at degree college level.

A few people made their researchers on the survey of textbooks. Their survey included on verifying various areas like the use of textbooks done by MSBT PCR (1974), appreciation of prose and poetry in the students by Banerji, (1980) and the position of women in school textbooks by Sarala Kumari (1996).

The related literature gathered from the studies done abroad revealed some work done in the areas of school textbooks. They included the studies based on printing technology by Willows (1978); moral judgement and moral values of students by Schuhler (1980), and Higgins (1980), and effects of religious education by Kathan (1971), Greeley and Gockel (1971), and Reynolds (1979). Some studies were done basing on vocabulary, form and functions of textbooks by Elson (1964), Huck (1965) and Solmon (1978).

On the whole, it can be seen that values have occupied a very primary interest of several researchers. Most of the findings have yielded positive results endorsing the beneficial and developmental role played by values in education by teachers at different levels of education informally, formally, and scientifically.

Method of Investigation

Several attempts have been made by researchers in identifying and locating required evidence on criterion measures. In fact, some of the researchers reported, squarely based their work on the analysis of textbooks at different levels using document analysis method.

To name a few, Pinge (1972), Linga Reddy (1987), Prasad (1991), MSBT PCR (1976), and Sarala Kumari (1996) have exclusively used the document analysis method. Prabhavathi (1994), Sathyavathi (1995), and Sai Leela (1996) also used the same research method in evaluating some general literature in Telugu language in realising certain values of education.

After establishing the research method, on the basis of the review of related literature on textbook evaluation, and in view of the aims of the present investigation, the following study procedures have been stipulated.

1. Preparation of the 'Value Manifestation Schedule' which details various ancillary contributors in the domain of the main values under consideration namely:

(a) Moral,

(b) Secular, and

(c) Democratic

2. A critical analysis of the textbook material applying the above schedule and quantifying the instances, evidences of occurrances of the value reflections in each of the lessons or chapters in the textbook.

3. A categorisation of the criterion occurrances standard wise, and in the three different forms of the language content, presentation namely:

   (a) Prose

   (b) Poetry, and

   (c) Non-detailed form

4. To classify the directness and indirectness or explicit and implicit nature in presenting the criterion.

5. Establishment of the extent of the incidence and intensity of the value references by classifying the data into:

   (a) Simple, and

   (b) Narrative and situation oriented

6. A classification of the instances of the induction of the values into chronological contexts, namely:

   (a) Contemporary and post independence period;

   (b) Historical and pre-independence period

The current problem in the state of Andhra Pradesh is that all the textbooks in primary and secondary stages are nationalised, i.e., state produced. They are periodically revised by experts through textbooks committees formed under the guidance of the State Council of Educational Research and Training (SCERT). The process of revision of textbooks at present in Andhra Pradesh is taking place from 1992.

Findings

The main findings of the study are:

1. Of the three values, there is more emphasis for moral value especially at secondary level than at the primary level.
2. The emphasis given to the democratic value is little less than average.
3. Comparatively, there is less emphasis on secular value with almost negligible emphasis at primary level.
4. Standard-wise, even emphasis was not given to the three values.

Moral Value

(a) The examination of the manifestation of the moral value in the lessons shows that the main focus of the lessons at primary level refer to good character, kindness and bravery.

(b) The manifestation of moral value at secondary level has its main focus on good character followed by the characteristics of selflessness, love and concern for others, and service mindedness.

(c) Literary form wise, the primary level textbooks are depending more on poetry form for presenting the moral value to the learner.

(d) At secondary level, while prose and poetry forms show equal emphasis for the presentation of moral value, nearly two thirds of the non-detailed content is used for presenting the moral value.

(e) Regarding the expression of moral value in the textbooks, i.e., explicit and implicit expressions, there are no reasons to conclude that the authors have preferred on type of expression over the other.

(f) The emphasis given to the type of expression is equally distributed between simple approach and narrative approach in primary level. But the same trend is not evident for the content at secondary level.

(g) The textual content at primary level is predominantly dependent on contemporary situation for presenting the moral value.

(h) The textual content at secondarily level gives equal emphasis to contemporary and historical periods for presenting moral value, but nearly four fifths of the non detailed lessons have utilised the historical situation to present the moral value.

Democratic Value

(a) The manifestation of democratic value in the textbooks analysed for this investigation shows that at primary level the main aspects that are emphasised are national integration followed by patriotism, equality and unity.

(b) At secondary level, the main focus with reference to democratic value is patriotism, freedom, justice and equality.

(c) In the literary form wise, the textbooks depend more upon poetry as a medium at primary level, whereas, this kind of difference is not much found in the second level textbooks.

(d) In terms of nature of expression, while there is variation at primary level, the secondary level books appear to be more balanced regarding the explicit and implicit expressions.

(e) In terms of the method of expression, i.e., simple vs. narrative and situation oriented approach, the secondary level books are giving actually the same emphasis for both the approaches. But, at primary level, nearly two thirds of the content in prose appears to be using narrative and situation oriented approach.

(f) In terms of the preference to the emphasis given to chronological periods, more than two thirds of the emphasis is given at the primary level lessons to post-independence period.

(g) On the whole, the main focus of the secondary level content is on pre-independence and historical period of inculcating the democratic value.

Secular Value

(a) Regarding the manifestations of secular value, both the primary and secondary level books are emphasising all the five manifestations of this value. The main focus of primary level books is on developing respect for all religions and duty towards society in a spirit of harmony. The secondary level books are basically emphasising respect for all religions followed by tolerance of other's view and duty to society.

(b) It terms of the literary form, the primary level content has used both prose and poetry with slightly increased emphasis in 5th standard.

(c) The presentation of secular value at secular level, is also not done in an orderly manner using all the literary forms. There does not seem to be appear a planned approach for using the literary form in presenting the secular value.

(d) Regarding the emphasis given to the expression of secular value in the implicit or explicit manner, the prose content at primary level is giving equal emphasis to both the approaches. Whereas, the poetry lessons at this level are totally dependent on explicit approach.

(e) At secondary level, three fourths of the prose content has used explicit approach. Whereas, two thirds of the non-detailed content is implicit in nature.

(f) Regarding the simple approach vs. narrative and situation oriented approach, the primary level content is mainly dependent on simple approach for presenting the secular value. At secondary level also, except in the content of non-detailed texts, the authors have dependend on simple approach for presenting the secular value.

(g) Regarding the use of chronological periods in presenting the secular value i.e. pre and post independence periods, the primary level content has given equal emphasis to both the pre and post independence periods.

(h) At secondary level, the prose lessons have given equal emphasis to both the periods.

(i) The poetry and non detailed content is mainly dependent on pre independence and historical periods for presenting the secular value.

Conclusion

It can be concluded from the value data classifications, that the inculcation of moral, democratic and secular value manifestations in the Telugu textbook is very dismal. Only moral value seems to have been given a semblance of some consideration.

Suggestions for Further Studies

On the basis of the findings of the research, further studies can be made on:

1. To evaluate the extent to which the students are exposed to the content or learning the values and their ramifications.

2. The extent to which the teachers, given the material with all its positive and negative aspects, are making deliberate and methodological efforts to conscentise the children in the value inculcations.

3. A study can also be undertaken to measure the additive or residual effects of other important agencies of education, like home, peer group, and mass media on the attainment of values by the children.

Bibliography

Ahlawat, S. (June-December, 1991), *Human Rights and Education*, Vol. 111, No. 2-4, NCTE Bulletin NCERT, New Delhi.

Ahmad, A. (1973). *A Study of Relationship Between Values and Modernity with Special Reference to College Girls*, Ph.D., Psy., Pat.U., Second Survey of Research in Education, NCERT, New Delhi.

Anitha Shetty, (December 1997), *Valuing Values*, Vol. 35, No. 52, University News, Association of Indian Universities, New Delhi.

Bell, (1976), *The International Encyclopaedia of Education*, Vol. 9, Pergamon Press, Oxford.

Benerjee, P.K., (1980), *A Study in the Appreciation of Prose and Poetry of Secondary School Children Ph.D Edu., Kal. U.*, Third Survey of Research in Education, NCERT, New Delhi.

Bertend Russell, (1961), *Education and the Social Order*, George Allen and Unwin Ltd., London.

Bhatnagar, I., (1984), *A Study of Some Family Characteristics as Related to Secondary School Student Activism, Values, Adjustment and School Learning*. Ph.D. Edu, Meerut University, Fourth Survey of Research in Education, NCERT, New Delhi.

Chandra Lekha, R.S. (December 1995), *Value Education for College Students*, University News, Association of Indian Universities, New Delhi.

Chandra Sekharaih, B.K. (1964), *An Investigation into the Basic Vocabulary of Elementary School Children of Standard I to VII of Mysore State*, Educational Research Bureau, Bangalore.

Chaudhari, I.S. (1977), *A Critical Evaluation of School Textbook Improvement Programmes in India*, Ph.D., Education, Punjab University, Second Survey of Research in Education, NCERT, New Delhi.

Chitty Babu, S.V. (May, 1997), *Convocation Address at Annamalai University*, Vol. 35, No. 8, University News, New Delhi.

Cronbach, (1995), *The Encyclopaedia of Education Research*, Fourth Edition, The Macmillan Company, Collier, Macmillan Ltd., London.

Dale and Chall (1948). *The International Encyclopaedia of Education*, Vol. 9, Pargamon Press, Oxford.

Daniel, J.T.K. (1990), *Value Education Today,* AIACHE, New Delhi.

Diwedi, C.B. (1983), *An Investigation into the Changing Social Values and Their Educational Implications*, Ph.D., Edu.; Gor. Uni., Fourth Survey of Research and Studies, Vol. 9, Pergamon Press, Oxford.

Gandhi, M.K. (January-March, 1974), *Gandhiji on Education,* Compiled by Rita Roy, Vol. IV. No. 2, New Frontiers in Education, AIACHE, New Delhi.

Gaur, R.S. (1975), *A Study of Values and Perceptions of High School Students of the State of Rajasthan and their Relation to Learning*, Ph.D. Edu.; Rajasthan University, Second Survey of Research in Education, NCERT, New Delhi.

Glen Langford and 'O' Cornor, D.J. (1973). *New Essays in the Philosophy of Education*, Routledge and Kegan Paul Ltd., London and Boston.

Gopaliah, G. (January-1981), *A Study of Moral Judgement in Children*, Vol. VIII, No. 11, Experiments in Education, New Delhi.

Gosh, N.G. (1977), *Distribution of Four Social Values Among Certain Selected Strata of Youths and Prediction of Good Citizenship with the Help of Values*, Ph.D., Education; Kal. University; Third Survey of Research of Education, NCERT, New Delhi.

Greeley, A.M.; and Gockel, G.L. (1971) *Encyclopaedia of Educational Research*, Fourth Volume, Fifth Edition, the Free Press, A Division of Macmillan Publishing Company, Inc., New York.

Higgins., (1980) *Hand Book of Research of Training,* Third Edition, Page—925, American Educational Research Association, Macmillan Publishing Company, Inc; New York.

Hilton, Ernest. (1969), *The Encyclopaedia of Educational Research,* Fourth Edition, The Macmillan Company, Collier, Macmillan Ltd., London.

Huck, (1965), *The International Encyclopaedia of Education Research and Studies*, Vol. 9, Page 1471, Pergamon Press, Oxford.

Jawaharlal Nehru, (1959)., *India and the World*, Azad Memorial Lectures, Indian Council of Cultural Relations, New Delhi.

John W. Best., (1982), *Research in Education,* Fourth Edition, Prentice Hall of India Private Ltd., New Delhi.

Kalia S., (1970), *Ego Ideals and Values of Students*, Ph.D., Psy, Agra, University; First Survey of Research in Education, NCERT, New Delhi.

Kathardekar, G.N. (1982), *A Study of Basic Vocabulary of Students Studying in Standard VII*, Ph.D, Edu; Poona Uni; Third Survey of Research in Education, NCERT, New Delhi.

Kireet Joshi. (1983), *Education for Human Values,* Compiled by Asha Sharma and Ahluwalia, S.P; Journal of Education for Allied Sciences, New Delhi.

Kluckhohn (1951), *The International Encyclopaedia of the Social Sciences,* Vol. 16, The Macmillan Company and the Free Press, New York, Collier, Macmillan Publishers, London.

Kothari, D.S., (1966), *Report of Education Commission*, Ministry of Education and Youth Services, Govt. of India, New Delhi.

Maharashtra *State Bureau of Textbook Production and Curriculum Research, MSBTPCR* (1974), State Wide Survey of Use of Textbooks, Third Survey of Research in Education, NCERT, New Delhi.

Margenau., (1959), *Education for Human Values,* Compiled by Asha Sharma and Ahluwalia, S.P. Page—84, Journal of Education and Allied Sciences, New Delhi.

Mascarenhas, M.M., (1983), *Family Life Education—Value Education*, AIACHE and CREST, New Delhi.

Mudaliyar, L.S., (1953), *Report of the Secondary Education Commission*, Ministry of Education, Govt. of India, Delhi.

Muthukumaran, S., (1991), *Issues in Higher Education, Science and Technology*, Published by Mrs. M. Ratan Vathi, Madras.

National Policy on Education, (1986), Ministry of Human Resource Development, The Challenge of Education Policy Perspective, Govt. of India, New Delhi.

Pandya, A.R.C., (1959), *Measurement of Modern Educational Values from Different Stand Points*, Ph.D., Education, Bombay University; First Survey of Research in Education, NCERT, New Delhi.

Patel, M.G., (1981), *A Study of the Prevalent Value System of the Students of South Gujarat Studying in Standards X and XI*, Ph.D., Education, S.G., University, Fourth Survey of Research in Education, NCERT, New Delhi.

Paul, P.V. (1986), *A Study of Value Orientations of Adolescent Boys and Girls*, Ph.D., Psy.; M.S. University; Fourth, Survey of Research in Education, NCERT, New Delhi.

Pinge, V.S., (1972), *A Critical Evaluation of Marathi Text Books for Standard V*, Ph.D., Education; Aurangabad University; The Survey of Research in Education, NCERT, New Delhi.

Pepper., (1958), *The International Encyclopaedia of the Social Sciences*, Vol. 16, The Macmillan Company and the Free Press, New York, Collier, Macmillan Publishers London.

Prabhavathy, G., (1974), *Study on Education Values in Children's Literature*, Ph.D., Education, Thesis submitted to Nagarjuna University, Andhra Pradesh.

Radha Krishnan, S., (1965), *Convocational Address*, As Cited in Vol. XL. No. 5, The Progress of Education, Delhi.

Reddy, V.N.K. (1976), *Education as a Medium of Integration of Value and Effective Value Changes*, Osmania University, Second Survey of Research in Education, NCERT, New Delhi.

Reynolds., (1979) *Encyclopaedia of Educational Research*, Fourth Volume, The Free Press, Macmillan Publishing Company, Inc., New York.

Rizvi, S.A.H., (1986), *A Study of Attitudes Towards Religious Education in Relation to Certain Value Orientations*, Ph.D., Psy; A.M. Uni; Fourth Survey of Research in Education, NCERT, New Delhi.

Rokeach, (Dec., 1997), Valuing Values, Compiled by Anitha Shetty, Vol. 35, No. 52, University News, New Delhi.

Ruhela, S.P., (1986), *Human Values and Education*, Sterling Publishers, Private Limited, New Delhi.

Sai Leela, K., (1996), *Realisation of Educational Values in the Ancient Sathakas*, Ph.D., Edu.; Thesis submitted to Nagarjuna University, Andhra Pradesh.

Sarala Kumari, K.L.S. (1996), *A Study of the Values Related to Women in the Secondary School Telugu Textbooks in Andhra Pradesh*, Ph.D., Edu.; Thesis submitted to S.P.M. University, Tirupati, A.P.

Saroj Bansal., (April 1981), *Values, Foundation of Curriculum*, Vol. LXXXVII, No. 4, The Educational Review, New Delhi.

Satyavathy, G., (1995), *Study of Educational Values in Telugu Novels,* Ph.D., Edu; Thesis submitted to Nagarjuna University, Andhra Pradesh.

Schuhler, (1980), *Hand Book of Research on Teaching*, Third Edition, Page—925, A Project of the American Educational Research Association, Macmillan Publishing Company, Inc, New York.

Seetha Ramu, A.S., (1974), *An Experimental Study of the Problem of Moral Instruction in Upper Primary Schools*, Ph.D., Edu; Mysore University; Second Survey of Research in Education, NCERT, New Delhi.

Sheila Kaul, (July—1983), *Objectives of the Teaching Profession*, Vol. XIII, No. 3, New Frontiers of Education, New Delhi.

Singh, R.P., (1960), *Democracy and Higher Secondary Education in Uttar Pradesh*, Ph.D.; Education; Luck, University; First Survey of Research in Education, New Delhi.

Singh, A.K., (1980), *Political Attitudes of College Students in Relation to Some Socio-Psychological Variables*, Ph.D., Psy.; Mag., University; Fourth Survey of Research in Education, New Delhi.

Solmon, M., (1978), *Encyclopaedia of Educational Research*, Fourth Volume, Fifth Edition, The Free Press, A Division of Macmillan Publishing Company, Inc., New York.

Sree Prakasa Committee on Religious and Moral Instruction, (1959), *Report of the Secondary Education Commission*, Government of India, New Delhi.

Tandon, B.K., (1967), *A Study of Attitudes Towards Religion of Higher Secondary School Students in U.P.* Ph.D., Edu; Agra University; First Survey of Research in Education, NCERT, New Delhi.

Tarlok Singh., (January—1983), *Educational Values of Literate and Illiterate Adults Belonging to Scheduled and Non Scheduled Castes*, Vol. 19, No. 3, Journal of Educational Research and Extension, New Delhi.

Titus., (1968), *Ethics for Today*, Eurasia Publication, Private Ltd., New Delhi, (Page 343).

Unninathan, T.K.N., (December—1988), *Education in Human Values*, University News, New Delhi.

Verma, (April, 1981), *Values—Foundation of Curriculum,* Compiled by Saroj Bansal, Vol. LXXXVII, No. 4, The Educational Review, New Delhi.

Zamen, G.S., (1982), *A Study of Social, Religious and Moral Values of Students of Class XI and their Relationship with Moral Character Traits and Personality Adjustment*, Ph.D., Edu., Avadh, University; Fourth Survey of Research in Education, NCERT, New Delhi.

Additional Reading

Bhaskara Rao, Digumarti (1994). *Scientific Aptitude*, New Delhi: Ashish Publishing House. ISBN 81-7024-658-X.

Bhaskara Rao, Digumarti (1995). *Animal Kingdom*. New Delhi: Discovery Publishing House. ISBN 81-7141-274-2.

Bhaskara Rao, Digumarti (1995). *Batracology*. New Delhi: Discovery Publishing House. ISBN 81-7141-279-3.

Bhaskara Rao, Digumarti (1996). *Scientific Attitude vis-à-vis Scientific Aptitude*. New Delhi: Discovery Publishing House. ISBN 81-7141-308-0.

Bhaskara Rao, Digumarti (2004). *Scientific Attitude, Scientific Apitude and Achievement*, New Delhi: Discovery Publishing House.

Bhaskara Rao, Digumarti, Editor (1996). *Encyclopaedia of Education for All,* 5 Volumes. New Delhi: APH Publishing Corporation. ISBN 81-7024-759-4 (set).

Vol. I *Education for All: The World Conference*. ISBN 81-7024-760-8.

Vol. II *Education for All: The EPA-9 Summit*. ISBN 81-7024-761-6.

Vol. III *Education for All: Quality Education for All*. ISBN 81-7024-762-6.

Vol. IV *Education for All: Planning and Monitoring.* ISBN 81-7024-763-4.

Vol. V *Education for All: The Indian Scenario.* ISBN 81-7024-764-0.

Bhaskara Rao, Digumarti, Editor (1996). *Global Perceptions on Peace Education,* 3 Volumes. New Delhi: Discovery Publishing House. ISBN 81-7141-319-6.

Bhaskara Rao, Digumarti, Editor (1996). *National Policy on Education.* 2 Volumes. New Delhi: Anmol Publications Pvt. Ltd. ISBN 81-7488-323-1.

Bhaskara Rao, Digumarti, Editor (1997). *Care the Child,* 2 Volumes. New Delhi: Discovery Publishing House. ISBN 81-7141-394-3.

Bhaskara Rao, Digumarti, Editor (1997). *Education for the 21st Century.* New Delhi: Discovery Publishing House. ISBN 81-7141-389-7.

Bhaskara Rao, Digumarti, Editor (1997). *Reflections on Scientific Attitude.* New Delhi: Discovery Publishing House, ISBN 81-7141-319-6.

Bhaskara Rao, Digumarti (1997). *Scientific Attitude.* New Delhi: Discovery Publishing House. ISBN 81-7141-381-1.

Bhaskara Rao, Digumarti, Editor (1997). *Success Story of a Primary Education Project.* New Delhi: APH Publishing Corporation. ISBN 81-7024-850-7.

Bhaskara Rao, Digumarti, Editor (1997). *World Food Summit.* New Delhi: Discovery Publishing House. ISBN 81-7141-386-2.

Bhaskara Rao, Digumarti, Editor (1998). *Adolescence Education.* New Delhi: Discovery Publishing House. ISBN 81-7141-432-X.

Bhaskara Rao, Digumarti, Editor (1998). *Community and School Nutrition Education.* New Delhi: Discovery Publishing House. ISBN 81-7141-435-4.

Bhaskara Rao, Digumarti, Editor (1998). *District Primary Education Programme.* New Delhi: Discovery Publishing House. ISBN 81-7141-396-X.

Bhaskara Rao, Digumarti, Editor (1998). *Earth Summit*, 2 Volumes. New Delhi: Discovery Publishing House. ISBN 81-7141-435-4.

Bhaskara Rao, Digumarti, Editor (1998). *National Policy on Education: Towards an Enlightened and Humane Society*, New Delhi: Discovery Publishing House. ISBN 81-7141-426-5.

Bhaskara Rao, Digumarti, Editor (1998). *Reforming School Education*. New Delhi: Discovery Publishing House. ISBN 81-7141-403-6.

Bhaskara Rao, Digumarti, Editor (1998). *Teacher Education in India*. New Delhi: Discovery Publishing House. ISBN 81-7141-406-0.

Bhaskara Rao, Digumarti, Editor (1998). *World Summit for Social Development*. New Delhi: Discovery Publishing House. ISBN 81-7141-420-6.

Bhaskara Rao, Digumarti, Editor (2000). *Education for All: Achieving the Goal*, 3 Volumes, New Delhi: APH Publishing Corporation. ISBN 81-7648-152-1.

Vol. I *The Global Consensus*. ISBN 81-7648-155-6.

Vol. II *Mid-Decade Review Reports of Regional Seminars*. ISBN 81-7648-154-8.

Vol. III *Issues and Trends*. ISBN 81-7648-155-6.

Bhaskara Rao, Digumarti, Editor (2000), *International Encyclopaedia of AIDS*, 11 Volumes in 13 Parts. New Delhi: Discovery Publishing House. ISBN 81-7141-6 (Set).

Vol. 1 *Introduction to HIV/AIDS*. ISBN 81-7141-523-7.

Vol. 2 *HIV/AIDS—Issues and Challenges*, 2 Parts. ISBN 81-7141-524-5.

Vol. 3 *HIV/AIDS—Socio Economic Realities*. ISBN 81-7141-524-3.

Vol. 4 *HIV/AIDS—Law Ethics and Human Rights*, 2 Parts. ISBN 81-7141-526-1.

Vol. 5 *AIDS and NGOs*. ISBN 81-7141-527-X.

Vol. 6 *AIDS and Home Care*. ISBN 81-7141-528-8.

Vol. 7 *STD Case Management*. ISBN 81-7141-529-6.

Vol. 8 *HIV/AIDS Prevention and Care—Teaching Modules for Nurses and Midwives*. ISBN 81-7141-530-X.

Vol. 9 *HIV Prevention Education for Education for Educational Institutions*. ISBN 81-7141-531-8.

Vol. 10 *Instructional Modules for AIDS Education*. ISBN 81-7141-532-6.

Vol. 11 *School Health Education to Prevent AIDS and STD—A Package for Curriculum Planners*. ISBN 81-7141-5338-4.

Bhaskara Rao, Digumarti, Editor (2000). *International Encyclopaedia of Science and Technology Education*, 11 Volumes. New Delhi: Discovery Publishing House. ISBN 81-7141-548-2 (Set).

Vol. 1 *Science and Technology Education*. ISBN 81-7141-568-7.

Vol. 2 *Science Education in Developing Countries*. ISBN 81-7141-570-9.

Vol. 3 *Organisational Structure of Science*. ISBN 81-7141-570-9.

Vol. 4 *Science Education in Asia and the Pacific*. ISBN 81-7141-571-7.

Vol. 5 *Science and Technology Education for All*. ISBN 81-7141-572-5.

Vol. 6 *Values, Ethics, Talent and Girls in Science and Technology Education*. ISBN 81-7141-573-3.

Vol. 7 *Popularisation of Science and Technology Education*. ISBN 81-7141-574-1.

Vol. 8 *Science, Power and Society*. ISBN 81-7141-575-X.

Vol. 9 *Information Technology*. ISBN 81-7141-576-8.

Vol. 10 *Teacher Training in Science and Technology Education*. ISBN 81-7141-577-6.

Vol. 11 *Teacher Training in Science and Technology: A Curriculum Framework*. ISBN 81-7141-578-4.

Bhaskara Rao, Digumarti, Editor (2001). *Distance Education in Different Countries*. New Delhi: APH Publishing Corporation. ISBN 81-7648-229-3.

Bhaskara Rao, Digumarti, Editor (2001). *Decentralised Management of Education (Management of Education in Panchayati Raj and Municipal Bodies)*. New Delhi: Discovery Publishing House. ISBN 81-7141-617-9.

Bhaskara Rao, Digumarti, Editor (2001). *Electrochemistry for Environmental Protection*. New Delhi: Discovery Publishing House. ISBN 81-7141-619-5.

Bhaskara Rao, Digumarti, Editor (2001). *Global Educational Studies*. New Delhi: Discovery Publishing House. ISBN 81-7141-616-0.

Bhaskara Rao, Digumarti, Editor (2001). *Global Synthesis of Educational Assessment*. New Delhi: Discovery Publishing House. ISBN 81-7141-613-6.

Bhaskara Rao, Digumarti, Editor (2000). *International Encyclopaedia of Human Rights*. 7 Volumes in 13 Parts. New Delhi: Discovery Publishing House. ISBN 81-7141-567-9 (Set).

Vol. 1 *International Instruments of Human Rights*, 2 Parts. ISBN 81-7141-595-4.

Vol. 2 *Regional Instruments of Human Rights*. ISBN 81-7141-604-7.

Vol. 3 *Human Rights and the United Nations*, 2 Parts. ISBN 81-7141-605-5.

Vol. 4 *Fact Files of Human Rights*, 3 Parts. ISBN 81-7141-605-3.

Vol. 5 *Study Stories of Human Rights*, 3 Parts. ISBN 81-7141-607-3.

Vol. 6 *International Meetings on Human Rights*, 2 Parts. ISBN 81-7141-608-X.

Vol. 7 *Professional Training in Human Rights*. ISBN 81-7141-609-8.

Bhaskara Rao, Digumarti, Editor (2001). *Jomtein Decade of Education*. New Delhi: Discovery Publishing House. ISBN 81-7141-618-7.

Bhaskara Rao, Digumarti, Editor (2001). *Nuclear Materials: Issues and Concerns*, 2 Volumes. New Delhi: Discovery Publishing House. ISBN 81-7141-611-X.

Bhaskara Rao, Digumarti, Editor (2001). *World Conference on Education for All*. New Delhi: APH Publishing Corporation. ISBN 81-7141-274-9.

Bhaskara Rao, Digumarti, Editor (2001). *World Conference on Higher Education*, New Delhi: Discovery Publishing House. ISBN 81-7141-610-1.

Bhaskara Rao, Digumarti, Editor (2001). *World Conference on Science*. New Delhi: Discovery Publishing House. ISBN 81-7141-612-8.

Bhaskara Rao, Digumarti, Editor (2004). *International Guidelines on Open and Distance Teacher Education*, New Delhi: Discovery Publishing House.

Bhaskara Rao Digumarti, Editor (2004). *Adult Learning in the 21st Century*, New Delhi: Discovery Publishing House.

Bhaskara Rao, Digumarti, Editor (2003). *Inspiring Experience in Teacher Education*. New Delhi: Discovery Publishing House. ISBN 81-7141-656-X.

Bhaskara Rao, Digumarti, Editor (2003). *International Studies in Education*, 3 Volumes, New Delhi: Discovery Publishing House. ISBN 81-7141-647-0. (Set).

Bhaskara Rao, Digumarti, Editor (2003). *Military Conversion: Impact on Science and Technology*, New Delhi: Discovery Publishing House. ISBN 81-7141-578-4.

Bhaskara Rao, Digumarti, Editor (2003). *Higher Education in the 21st Centuery: Vision and Action*, New Delhi: Discovery Publishing House.

Bhaskara Rao, Digumarti, Editor (2003). *United Nations Millennium Summit*. New Delhi: Discovery Publishing House. ISBN 81-7141-632-2.

Bhaskara Rao, Digumarti, Editor (2003). *World Assembly on Aging*. New Delhi: Discovery Publishing House. ISBN 81-7141-637-3.

Bhaskara Rao, Digumarti, Editor (2003). *World Conference on Human Rights*. New Delhi: Discovery Publishing House. ISBN 81-7141-661-6.

Bhaskara Rao, Digumarti, Editor (2003). *World Education Forum*. New Delhi: Discovery Publishing House. ISBN 81-7141-639-X.

Bhaskara Rao, Digumarti, Editor (2003). *Education Employment and Human Resource Development*. New Delhi: Discovery Publishing House. ISBN 81-7141-681-0.

Bhaskara Rao, Digumarti, Editor (2004). *Learning to Live Together*, 4 Volumes. New Delhi: Discovery Publishing House.

Bhaskara Rao, Digumarti, Editor (2004). *Successful Schooling*. New Delhi: Discovery Publishing House. ISBN 81-7141-677-2.

Bhaskara Rao, Digumarti, Editor (2004). *European Education and Teachers*. New Delhi: Discovery Publishing House. ISBN 81-7141-702-7.

Bhaskara Rao, Digumarti, Editor (2004). *Teachers in a Changing World*. New Delhi: Discovery Publishing House. ISBN 81-7141-694-2.

Bhaskara Rao, Digumarti, Editor (2003). *Education: Policies and Programmes*. New Delhi: APH Publishing Corporation. ISBN 81-7648-470-9.

Bhaskara Rao, Digumarti, C.A.P. Swami and B.S.V. Dutt (1997). *Self-Evaluation in Student Teaching*. New Delhi: Discovery Publishing House. ISBN 81-7141-374-9.

Bhaskara Rao, Digumarti and Digumarti Pushpa Latha (1994). *Achievement in Biology*. New Delhi: Discovery Publishing House. ISBN 81-7141-264-5.

Bhaskara Rao, Digumarti, C. Sridevi and K. Vijaya (1995). *Achievement in Social Studies*. New Delhi: Discovery Publishing House. ISBN 81-7141-281-5.

Bhaskara Rao, Digumarti and Digumarti Pushpa Latha (199 *Achievement in English*. New Delhi: Discovery Pu House. ISBN 81-7141-283-1.

Bhaskara Rao, Digumarti and Digumarti Pushpa Latha (1994). *Achievement in Science*. New Delhi: Discovery Publishing House. ISBN 81-7141-280-70.

Bhaskara Rao, Digumarti and Digumarti Pushpa Latha (1995). *Achievement in Mathematics*. New Delhi: Discovery Publishing House. ISBN 81-7141-278-5.

Bhaskara Rao, Digumarti and Digumarti Pushpa Latha, Editors (1998). *International Encyclopaedia of Women*. 5 Volumes. New Delhi: Discovery Publishing House. ISBN 81-7141-410-9.

Vol. 1 *Status of World's Women*. ISBN 81-7141-494-X.

Vol. 2 *Women, Education and Empowerment*. ISBN 81-7141-498-1.

Vol. 3 *Women Challenges and Advancement*. ISBN 81-7141-497-4.

Vol. 4 *Women and Family Health*. ISBN 81-7141-497-4.

Vol. 5 *Women and International Action*. ISBN 81-7141-498-2.

Bhaskara Rao, Digumarti, Digumarti Pushpa Latha and Digumarti Harshitha, Editors (2001). *Biological Warfare*. New Delhi: Discovery Publishing House. ISBN 81-7141-597-0.

Bhaskara Rao, Digumarti, Digumarti Pushpa Latha and Digumarti Harshitha, Editors (2001). *Women as Educators*. New Delhi: Discovery Publishing House. ISBN 81-7141-602-0.

Bhaskara Rao, Digumarti and Digumarti Harshitha, Editors (2001). *Education in India*. New Delhi: APH Publishing Corporation. ISBN 81-7846-207-2.

Bhaskara Rao, Digumarti, Digumarti Pushpa Latha and Digumarti Harshitha, Editors (2001). *Assessing Learning Achievement*. New Delhi: Discovery Publishing House. ISBN 81-7141-601-2.

Bhaskara Rao, Digumarti, Digumarti Pushpa Latha and Digumarti Harshitha, Editors (2001). *Energy Security*. New Delhi: Discovery Publishing House. ISBN 81-7141-598-9.

Bhaskara Rao, Digumarti, Digumarti Harshitha and K.R.S.S. Rao, Editors (1999). *Advanced Biotechnology*. New Delhi: Discovery Publishing House. ISBN 81-7141-516-4.

Bhaskara Rao, Digumarti and D. Sridhar (2002). *Job Satisfaction of School Teachers*. New Delhi: Discovery Publishing House. ISBN 81-7141-652 7.

Bhaskara Rao, Digumarti and K.R.S. Sambhasiva Rao, Editors (1996). *Current Trends in Indian Education*. New Delhi: Discovery Publishing House. ISBN 81-7141-311-0.

Bhaskara Rao, Digumarti and K. Vijaya (1995). *A Text Book of Evaluation*. Ambala Cantt: The Associated Publishers.

Bhaskara Rao, Digumarti and N.V.M. Mohana Rao (2002). *Problems of Mentally Handicapped Children*. New Delhi: Discovery Publishing House. ISBN 81-7141-645-4.

Bhaskara Rao, Digumarti and S. Chandra Mohan (2002). *Sports Management*. New Delhi: APH Publishing Corporation. ISBN 81-7648-467-9.

Bhaskara Rao, Digumarti and Sk. Basha (2004). *Teachers' Population Educaton Awareness*. New Delhi: Discovery Publishing House.

Bhaskara Rao, Digumarti, V.V. Rao, V.V. Lakshmi and V.V. Krishna, Editors (1999). *Status and Advancement of Women*. New Delhi: APH Publishing Corporation. ISBN 81-7648-169-6.

Babu, P.C., Author and Digumarti Bhaskara Rao, Editor (2004). *Flowers of Wisdom*. New Delhi: Discovery Publishing House. ISBN 81-7141-695-0.

Bhagya Lakshmi, Lingineni, Author and Digumarti Bhaskara Rao, Editor (2000). *Reading and Comprehension*. New Delhi: Discovery Publishing House. ISBN 81-7141-543-1.

Bhuvaneswara Lakshmi, Gadde, Author and Digumarti Bhaskara Rao, Editor (2000). *Attitude Towards Science*. New Delhi: Discovery Publishing House. ISBN 81-7141-541-6.

Devraj, T.A.S., Author and Digumarti Bhaskara Rao, Editor (1997). *Trace Analysis of Uranium and Thorium*. New Delhi: Discovery Publishing House. ISBN 81-7141-375-7.

Durga Rani, K., Author and Digumarti Bhaskara Rao, Editor (2000). *Educational Aspirations and Scientific Attitudes*. New Delhi: Discovery Publishing House. ISBN 81-7141-555-55.

Dutt, B.S.V. and Digumarti Bhaskara Rao (2001). *Empowering Primary Teachers*. New Delhi: Discovery Publishing House. ISBN 81-7141-615.2.

Ediger, Marlow and Digumarti Bhaskara Rao (1996). *Science Curriculum*. New Delhi: Discovery Publishing House. ISBN 81-7141-321-8.

Ediger, Marlow and Digumarti Bhaskara Rao (2000). *Teaching Mathematics Successfully*. New Delhi: Discovery Publishing House. ISBN 81-7141-552-0.

Ediger, Marlow and Digumarti Bhaskara Rao (2001). *Teaching Science Successfully*. New Delhi: Discovery Publishing House. ISBN 81-7141-600-4.

Ediger, Marlow and Digumarti Bhaskara Rao (2001). *Teaching Social Studies Successfully*. New Delhi: Discovery Publishing House. ISBN 81-7141-596-2.

Ediger, Marlow and Digumarti Bhaskara Rao (2002). *Philosophy and Curriculum*. New Delhi: Discovery Publishing House. ISBN 81-7141-631-4.

Ediger, Marlow and Digumarti Bhaskara Rao (2002). *Improving School Administration*. New Delhi: Discovery Publishing House. ISBN 81-7141-633-0.

Ediger, Marlow and Digumarti Bhaskara Rao (2002). *Elementary Curriculum*. New Delhi: Discovery Publishing House. ISBN 81-7141-658-6.

Ediger, Marlow and Digumarti Bhaskara Rao (2003). *Language Arts Curriculum*. New Delhi: Discovery Publishing House. ISBN 81-7141-657-8.

Ediger, Marlow and Digumarti Bhaskara Rao (2003). *Elementary Curriculum Improvement,* New Delhi: Discovery Publishing House. ISBN 81-7141-740-X.

Ediger, Marlow and Digumarti Bhaskara Rao (2003). *Psychology and Curriculum*. New Delhi: Discovery Publishing House. ISBN 81-7141-691-8.

Ediger, Marlow and Digumarti Bhaskara Rao (2003). *Teaching Language Arts Successfully*. New Delhi: Discovery Publishing House. ISBN 81-7141-678-0.

Ediger, Marlow and Digumarti Bhaskara Rao (2003). *Teaching Mathematics in Elementary Schools*. New Delhi: Discovery Publishing House. ISBN 81-7141-687-X.

Ediger, Marlow and Digumarti Bhaskara Rao (2003). *Teaching Science in Elementary Schools*. New Delhi: Discovery Publishing House. ISBN 81-7141-698-5.

Ediger, Marlow and Digumarti Bhaskara Rao, (2003). *Teaching Social Studies in Elementary Schools*. New Delhi: Discovery Publishing House.

Ediger, Marlow and Digumarti Bhaskara Rao (2003). *School Curriculum and Administration*. New Delhi: Discovery Publishing House. ISBN 81-7141-709-4.

Ediger, Marlow and Digumarti Bhaskara Rao (2004): *Relevancy in Elementary Curriculum*. New Delhi: Discovery Publishing House. ISBN 81-7141-751-5.

Ediger Marlow, B.S.V. Dutt and Digumarti Bhaskara Rao (2003). *Teaching English Successfully*. New Delhi: Discovery Publishing House. ISBN 81-7141-707-8.

Jayasree, Kandi, Author and Digumarti Bhaskara Rao, Editor (1999). *Correlates of Socialisation*. New Delhi: Discovery Publishing House. ISBN 81-7141-517-2.

John Babu, Chikati, Author and T.J.R. Prasad, G.M. Madhukar and Digumarti Bhaskara Rao, Editors (1996). *Problem Solving in Mathematics*. New Delhi: APH Publishing Corporation. ISBN 81-7648-273-0.

Jyothi Nirmala, M., Author and Digumarti Bhaskara Rao, Editor (2003). *Non-detention Systems in School Education*. New Delhi: Discovery Publishing House. ISBN 81-7141-654-3.

Marja, Talvi and Digumarti Bhaskara Rao, Editors (1996). *Educational Leadership and Social Changes*. New Delhi: Discovery Publishing House. ISBN 81-7141-320-X.

Prabhakaram, K.S., Author and Digumarti Bhaskara Rao, Editor (1998). *Concept Attainment Model in Mathematics Teaching*. New Delhi: Discovery Publishing House. ISBN 81-7141-424-9.

Prasanth Kumar, J., Author and Digumarti Bhaskara Rao, Editor (1998). *Effectiveness of Distance Education System*. New Delhi: Discovery Publishing House. ISBN 81-7141-437-0.

Prasanth Kumar, J., Author and G. Sundara Rao and Digumarti Bhaskara Rao, Editors (2000). *Open University Student Support Services*. New Delhi: Discovery Publishing House. ISBN 81-7141-550-4.

Ramatulasamma, K., Author and Digumarti Bhaskara Rao, Editor (2002). *Job Satisfaction of Teacher Educators*, New Delhi: Discovery Publishing House. ISBN 81-7141-655-1.

Rama Krishnaiah, D., Author and Digumarti Bhaskara Rao, Editor (1998). *Job Satisfaction of College Teachers*, New Delhi: Discovery Publishing House. ISBN 81-7141-438-9.

Rathaiah, Lavu and Digumarti Bhaskara Rao, Editors (1996). *International Innovations in Education*. New Delhi: Discovery Publishing House. ISBN 81-7141-359-5.

Ramesh, Ganta and Digumarti Bhaskara Rao, Editors (1998). *Environmental Education: Problems and Prospects*. New Delhi: Discovery Publishing House. ISBN 81-7141-423-0.

Ramkumar Ratnam, M., Author and Digumarti Bhaskara Rao, Editor (2003). *Dukkha: Suffering in Early Buddhism*. New Delhi: Discovery Publishing House.

Rathaiah, Lavu and Digumarti Bhaskara Rao (1997). *Achievement Correlates.* New Delhi: Discovery Publishing House. ISBN 81-7141-385-4.

Reddy, Sudhakar Y., Author, and Digumarti Bhaskara Rao, Editor (2003). *Creativity in Adolescents.* New Delhi: Discovery Publishing House. ISBN 81-7141-659-4.

Reddy, M.S., Author and Digumarti Bhaskara Rao, Editor (2003). *Creativity in College Students.* New Delhi: Discovery Publishing House. ISBN 81-7141-697-7.

Rudramamba, B., Author and Digumarti Bhaskara Rao, Editor (2003). *Problems of Teaching.* New Delhi: APH Publishing Corporation. ISBN 81-7648-462-8.

Sanjeeva Rao, P.C., Author and Digumarti Bhaskara Rao, Editor (1996). *A Text Book of Geology.* New Delhi: Discovery Publishing House. ISBN 81-7141-313-7.

Satya Narayana V., Author and Digumarti Bhaskara Rao, Editor (2001). *Physical Education, Social Attitudes and Leadership Qualities.* New Delhi: Discovery Publishing House. ISBN 81-7141-593-8.

Srinivasulu Reddy, M., and K.R.S. Sambasiva Rao, Authors and Digumarti Bhaskara Rao, Editor (1999). *A Text Book of Aquaculture.* New Delhi: Discovery Publishing House. ISBN 81-7141-482-6.

Srinivasa Rao, Mandalapu, Author and Digumarti Bhaskara Rao, Editor (2003). *Achievement Motivation and Achievement in Mathematics.* New Delhi: Discovery Publishing House. ISBN 81-7141-674-8.

Vanaja, M. Author and Digumarti Bhaskara Rao, Editor (1999). *Inquiry Training Model.* New Delhi: Discovery Publishing House. ISBN 81-7141-515-6.

Vanaja. M. N. Sneha Latha, and Digumarti Bhaskara Rao, Editor (2003). *Student Shyness.* New Delhi: APH Publishing Corporation.

Valeri V. Koustiouk, Author and Digumarti Bhaskara Rao, Editor (2002). *A Text Book of Cryogenics*. New Delhi: Discovery Publishing House. ISBN 81-7141-642-X.

Valeri V. Koustiouk, Author and Digumarti Bhaskara Rao, Editor (2003). *Refrigeration and Environment*. New Delhi: APH Publishing Corporation.

Veena Kumari, Balusu and Digumarti Bhaskara Rao (1996). *Operation Black Board*. New Delhi: Discovery Publishing House. ISBN 81-7141-711-X.

Veena Kumari, Balusu, Author and Digumarti Bhaskara Rao, Editor (2000). *Psycho-Social Correlates of Achievement*, New Delhi: Discovery Publishing House. ISBN 81-7141-547-4.

Venkata Rao, P. and Digumarti Bhaskara Rao (1989). *A Text Book of Zoology—Junior Intermediate*. Guntur: Vignan Publishers.

Venkata Rao, P. and Digumarti Bhaskara Rao (1989). *A Text Book of Zoology—Senior Intermediate*. Guntur: Vignan Publishers.

Venugopala Rao, K., Author and Digumarti Bhaskara Rao, Editor (2000). *Teacher Morale in Secondary Schools*. New Delhi: Discovery Publishing House. ISBN 81-7141-551-2.

Vidya, C., Author and Digumarti Bhaskara Rao. Editor (1996). *A Text Book of Nutrition*. New Delhi: Discovery Publishing House. ISBN 81-7141-309-9.

Vijaya Bharathi, D., Author and Digumarti Bhaskara Rao, Editor (2000). *Educational Philosophies of Swami Vivekananda and John Dewey*. New Delhi: APH Publishing Corporation. ISBN 81-7648-309-9.

Books in Telugu Language

Bhaskara Rao, Digumarti (1986). *Dhrushya Sravana Bodhanapakaranalu* (Audio Visual Teaching Aids). Guntur: Nagarjuna Publishers.

Bhaskara Rao, Digumarti (1993). *Jeevasashtra Bodhana* (Teaching of Biology). Guntur: Nagarjuna Publishers.

Bhaskara Rao, Digumarti (1995). *Vignanasasthra Bodhana* (Teaching of Science) Guntur: Nagarjuna Publishers.

Bhaskara Rao, Digumarti (1997). *Vidya Manovignana Seshtram* (Educational Psychology). Guntur: Creative Press.

Bhaskara Rao, Digumarti (1998). *DSC Study Material*. Guntur: Nagarjuna Publishers.

Bhaskara Rao, Digumarti (1998). *Upadhyayudu Vidya*. (Teacher and Education). Guntur: Nagarjuna Publishers.

Bhaskara Rao, Digumarti (1998). *Vidya Drukpadalu* (Prespectives of Education). Guntur: Nagarjuna Publishers.

Bhaskara Rao, Digumarti (1999). *EdCET Teaching Aptitude*. Guntur: Nagarjuna Publishers.

Bhaskara Rao, Digumarti (2001). *Bharata Samajamulo Upadyayudu Vidya* (Teacher and Education in Emerging Indian Society). Guntur: Nagarjuna Publishers.

Bhaskara Rao, Digumarti (2001). *Bhoutika Sastra Bodhana Paddathulu* (Methods of Teaching Physical Science). Guntur: Nagarjuna Publishers.

Bhaskara Rao, Digumarti (2001). *Jeeva Sastra Bodhana Padhathulu* (Methods of Teaching Biology). Guntur: Nagarjuna Publishers.

Bhaskara Rao, Digumarti (2001). *Vidya Manovignana Sastram* (Educational Psychology). Guntur: Nagarjuna Publishers.

Bhaskara Rao, Digumarti (2003). *Patsala Yajamanyam / Paripalana* (School Management and Administration). Guntur: Nagarjuna Publishers.

Bhaskara Rao, Digumarti (2004). *Vidya Sanketika Sastram mariyu Computer Vidya* (Educational Technology and Computer Education). Guntur: Nagarjuna Publishers.

Index

A

Achievement orientation, 38
Agencies of social change, 41
Ahlawat, S., 6
Ahmad, S., 38, 145
Aims and values of education, 2
Aligarh Muslim University, 45
Ambedkar, Dr. B.R., 78, 105, 124
Animuthyalu, 73
Artha, 2
Azad, Moulana Abul Kalam, 109, 118

B

Babu, Chitty, 16
Bai, Lakshmi, 74
Bai, Sangam Lakshmi, 102
Bai, Unnava Lakshmi, 95
Bala Seva Snagham, 74
Banerji, 147
Bansal, Saroj, 13
Bell, 62
Benerji, P.K., 53
Best, J.W., 61
Bhatnagar, I., 43
Birth order, 43
Bondu Mallelu, 75
Broken family, 43
Bujji Meka, 88

C

Carey, William, 85, 94
Chall, 61
Chandrasekharaiah, 50
Chaudhari, I.S., 51, 146
Classification of values, 12, 141
  national values, 18
  personal values, 14-15
  social values, 16
College adolescents, 44
Cotton, Sir Arthur, 90
Cronbach, 25
Cultural values, 23
Curriculum of education, 39

D

Dale, 61
Democratic values, 97, 116, 150
Description of documents, 64
Devaluation in the personality, 39
Developing law, 75
Diwedi, C.B., 39, 145
Duties of citizen, 112

E

Eclectic expression used, 33
Economic, 45
Education Commission report, 9

Education system, 30
Educational level of the family, 38
Elson, 147
Explicit, 33

F

Fashim mindedness, 38
Fry, 61

G

Gaur, R.S., 41, 145
Girls scored higher than the boys on rational values, 42
Gockel, G.L., 56, 147
Gopaliah, G., 46, 47
Gosh, N.G., 41, 145
Greatest influence, 42
Greeley, A.M., 56
Group of respondents, 39

H

Higgins, 58, 147
Hiltn, Ernest, 26
Hindu communities, 45
Huck, 55, 147
Humanistic values, 43

I

Implicit, 33
Importance of developing, 100
Incomplete Sentence Bank (ISB), 40
Innumerable imperfections at every level, 39

J

Jalot's Group, 45

K

Kalia, S., 145
Kanuvippu, 75
Kastha Jeevi, 133
Kathan, 55
Kaul, Shiela, 12
Klare, 61
Kluchohn, 7
Knowledge, 39
Kothari Education Commission (1964-66), 5, 25, 30
Krause, 62
Kumari, Sarala, 54, 61

L

Language and literature, 31
Leela, Sai, 49, 61
Lekha, Chandra, 8
Lessons at secondary level, 112
Library bulletin, 55
Literary form wise, 150
Low democratic-oriented students, 49
Lower income group, 45

M

Male adolescents, 44
Malleu, Bondu, 89
Mana Panini Maname Chesukundam, 101
Manifestation of democratic value, 150
Mascarenhas, 12
Meaning of values, 7
Meints, 62
Melasi, Kalasi, 99
Method of investigation, 147
Moksha, 2
Moral values, 71, 92, 149
– – of students, 42
Mudaliayar Education Commission (1953), 3

Muslim communities, 45
Muthukumaran, 8
Mysore district, 46

N

National Education Policy (1986), 10, 11, 30
Nature of offering something, 75
Nayakar, Sree Sathya Lingam, 86
Nidra, Urmila Devi, 81, 93
Nizam government, 114
Non-detailed texts, 90, 93, 96, 107

O

Old values, 39

P

Panduga, Puttina Roju, 101
Pandya, 38, 145
Parental occupation, 38
Pata, Ankela, 99
Patel, 42, 91, 146
Patle, Sardar Vallabha Bhai, 84
Paul, 44
Pepper, 7, 141
Personality adjustment inventory, 42
Pillalu, Kavala, 89
Pinge, 60, 146, 147
Place of residence, 39
Place of value in education, 69
Poetry lessons, 93
Poolu, Muddabanthi, 122
Positively and significantly influenced by values, 43
Prabhavathy, 49, 61, 146
Prapacha Santhi (world peace), 75, 107
Prasa Vakyalu, 73
Prasad, 61, 146, 147
Present system of education, 39
Primary level, 73, 87, 95, 98
- school teachers, 50
Process of modern social change, 40

Q

Qualitative interpretation, 68, 71

R

Rao, Jamalapuram Kesava, 78
Rao, K.L., 113, 117, 128
Rao, Kashmana, 125
Rao, Sardar Jamalapuram Kesava, 88, 102
Rao, Subba, 86, 91
Rayalu, Sree Krishna Deva, 131
Realisation of educational, 49
Reddy, C.L., 131, 145
Reddy, Linga, 60
Reddy, Pratapa, 88
Reddy, S.C., 114
Reddy, Sir C.R., 108
Reddy, Suravaram Prathapa, 102, 104
Religions values, 43
Respect to social values, 44
Reynolds, 57
Rizvi, S.A.H., 45, 146
Rokeach, 7, 141
Role of textbook, 24-36
explanation of the important term used, 33
democratic values, 34

eclectic expression, 35
explicit and implicit expressions, 35
moral values, 34
mother tongue textbooks, 34
school level, 35
secular values, 34
simple and narrative expression, 36
value, 33
- education, 33
need and importance of the study, 29
scope of limitation of the study, 33, 145
teaching of language, 24
textbooks in mother tongue, 27
Rural boys, 41
- girls, 41

S

Sahakaram, 75
Samaikya Bharathi, 113
Santhi, Prapancha, 93
Sathyavathy, 49
Satyavathi, 146
Schuhler, 57
Secondary education, 30
- level, 75, 96
- schools documents, 66
Secular value, 151
Seshan, T.N., 6
Singh, A.K., 48, 146
Singh, Tarlok, 40
Size of the family effected student activism, 43
Social and moral values, 41, 43
Socio-economic status, 43
Solmon, 57, 147
Sources of value education, 20, 143
Sri Prakasa Committee (1959), 30, 142
State Council of Educational Research and Training (SCERT), 148
State-wide survey of use of textbooks, 52
Studies abroad, 55
- of religious values, 44
- - value of students, 40
- on democratic values, 47
- - evaluation a textbooks, 51
- - measurement of educational values, 49
- - moral instruction, 46
- - survey of textbooks, 52
- - value in education in general, 38
- - - - textbooks, 50
Study of attitudes towards religion of higher secondary school student of Uttar Pradesh, 45
Study on value orientations of adolescent boys, 44
Subhashitalu, 73

T

Tandon, 44, 45, 146
Telugu language textbooks, 59, 67
Terminal values, 44
Test of General Mental Ability, 48
Type of fluctuations, 70

U

University Education Commission (1948), 3, 4, 30
Urban adolescents, 44
Urban boy, 41
– girls, 41
Usha, P.T., 84, 90

V

Value education, 9, 141
– manifestation schedule, 33, 63
Values lead the investigator, 70
Verman, 22

W

Willows, 58, 147
World peace, 78, 107

Y

Youth of the highest socio-economic, 41

Z

Zaman, 42